SCHUTZHUND OBEDIENCE
Training in Drive

ALSO BY SHEILA BOOTH

PURELY POSITIVE TRAINING
Companion to Competition

THE POSITIVE PUPPY PREVIEW
(Audiocassette on puppy evaluation)

SCHUTZHUND OBEDIENCE
Training in Drive

with
Gottfried Dildei

by
Sheila Booth

Podium Publications

PODIUM PUBLICATIONS
P.O. Box 32, Free Union, Va. 22940
onpodium@optonline.net

ISBN 0-9663020-2-8

Tenth Printing - Year 2006
Printed in the U.S.A.
Printed on recycled paper at
The Royal Fireworks Press
Unionville, NY

For Ingrid.
— G.D.

For Gypsy,
who made me a dog trainer.
— S.B.

CONTENTS

FOREWORD ix
PREFACE xi

1 Why? 1
2 How? 7
3 Drives 25
4 Corrections 43
5 Getting Started 55
6 Happy Heeling 67
7 The Solid Sit 119
8 Sit in Motion 135
9 Dynamic Down 149
10 Focused Front 167
11 The Racing Recall 181
12 Front to Finish 189
13 Rocket Retrieves 199
14 Up and Over 215
15 The Flying Voraus 231
16 Long Distance Down 245
17 Steady Stands 257
18 Putting It All Together 275

GLOSSARY xvii
PHOTO INFORMATION xxi
ABOUT THE AUTHORS xxvi
ACKNOWLEDGEMENTS xxxi

FOREWORD

Finally, here's a motivational manual for trainers who really like their dogs. *Training In Drive* teaches your dog to enjoy working. And here's a way you can actually have fun while training!

This method gives your dog choices. Then you simply reward your dog for making the correct choice.

Here are techniques that give our dogs credit for being intelligent, sensitive creatures who enjoy working when we allow them to think for themselves. This happy attitude assures your dog will work joyfully and correctly many more years than any force training can ever produce.

Most working dogs love to work. Desire to please is part of their very nature. Given the choice, they choose to work – and to work happily. These techniques allow them to maintain that happy attitude!

Motivational training not only allows your dog to think, it actually encourages him to think. Once your dog figures it out for himself, he enjoys his work even more.

Once your dog knows how to get what he wants from you, the work becomes more and more rewarding for him. You allow your dog to be creative until he learns how to be correct. Immediate reward when he gets it right makes him want to continue working for you and with you.

Here's a way that allows your dog to use all his natural capabilities. He solves problems and makes his own choices. If you're tired of underestimating your dog, then this is the way for you.

Many of the techniques are based on scientific principles of learning and behavior. Most were pioneered in the training of sea mammals, using the most fundamental, universally accepted "motivational" teaching methods. You can't put a prong collar on a killer whale and live to tell about it! When you use similar motivational techniques, your dog learns to enjoy training, loves his work and loves working for you and with you.

Confusion and conflict disappear. The way is clear for your dog. Here's a way to train without coercion, without bribery or unfair corrections. When your dog does it right, he gets what he wants.

If you enjoy jerking your dog around and correcting him before he even knows what to do, then this method may not be for you. This training allows your dog to be wrong, but then rewards him for figuring out what's right.

If you are looking for a quick fix, then these techniques may not be for you. This training relies on creating the correct habit, and then building your dog's expectation of reward. It works. But it can take more time to see results in the beginning, while building a strong foundation.

Here's a way that offers you and your dog the pleasure of teamwork. Here's a way that creates harmony through understanding and trust. Here's a way that sees training from the dog's point of view.

Here's a method and a book that rely heavily on the positive. If you're looking for a way to have real fun with your dog while training, here it is.

Our only hope is that you and your dog find it as rewarding as we have. Happy Reading and Happy Training!

– Mary Lou Brayman
1990 Deutsche Meister
with her Malinois, Igor

PREFACE

We Salute . . .

— the founder of modern training, Col. Konrad Most, whose principles remain as vital today as they did more than 40 years ago when *Training Dogs* was first published, even though his methods have been modified.

— all those who help us better understand our dogs by their dedication to the study of animal ethology and behavior, especially of wolves.

— all the working dog organizations (both here and abroad), for developing our dogsport and providing a standard to evaluate temperament for breeding suitability, as well as a place for us all to compete in an enjoyable sport with our canine companions.

— all those who work with service dogs, training and using them to assist people within our society, such as police K-9s, guide dogs for the blind, search and rescue dogs, hearing ear dogs and companion dogs for the disabled, therapy dogs, Armed forces dogs, customs screening dogs and bomb detection dogs.

– G.D. & S.B.

*We are in luck if, in training a dog, we can use
his instincts as a basis for what we require.
For the more instinctive an action is,
the more reliable it will be.*

– Konrad Most

SCHUTZHUND OBEDIENCE
Training in Drive

1. ATTENTION.

Chapter 1

Why?

*All knowledge, the totality of all questions
and all answers, is contained in the dog.*
— Franz Kafka

The question is why we need a new approach to training. The answer is because we want to achieve the highest possible

Attention + Attitude + Accuracy.

Attention is generated by making yourself (the handler) the most interesting thing to your dog.
Attitude comes from working with the dog's drives so training becomes enjoyable for your dog.
Accuracy results when discipline reinforces correct habits through the dog's *drive*.

This "Triple A Training" is the goal of students here at The Whatever Works School of Dog Training. We have tried many ways to attain these three essential elements of successful obedience.

Acceptable **Accuracy** is common. And we can get a

1

dog's **Attention** several ways. But an enthusiastic **Attitude** remained the most elusive – until now.

We believe a working dog should **enjoy** obedience. We thrill to see a dog who is as exciting (and excited) in obedience as in protection.

We aspire to see our dogs come on the recall nearly as fast as they do on the courage test. When we train the dog through his drives, he becomes both attentive and accurate, as well as a joy to train and to watch.

So here we base our training on the dog's **desire** to work. As your dog learns what you expect, he finds out how to get what he wants from you (the handler).

The dog now gets to control what happens to him. He brings **spirit** and **enthusiasm** to his work. He starts out with the right **Attitude**.

Training becomes fun and enjoyable for the dog. This makes training fun for us too!

The Foundation

Building a motivational **Foundation** takes time. But this proper foundation is the key to training that lasts.

To maintain the dog's enthusiasm, there must **always** be something in it for the dog (unless you find one who works for money). Thus you must discover what makes the work **exciting** to your dog.

Training in this manner is like building a road – the quality and lifespan of both depend on the proper layers of **Foundation**. Both need a destination; and both need a plan.

Both encounter obstacles that require detours. The road is not smooth, nor straight, while under construction. You need to slow down at the unexpected curves!

But when you paint that final center line on a road with a strong foundation, it remains smooth and straight for years with only minor maintenance. So your dog's training holds fast much longer when the **Foundation** is correct.

Working in Drive

To train any dog, he **must** have the *drive* for the activity. For our purposes, *drive* is the dog's pronounced desire to persist in certain behavior. Our working dogs have been bred selectively to produce strong drives for tracking, retrieving, fighting, chasing (*prey drive*) and playing, among others.

Activating the dog's *drive* is fundamental to motivational training. **Building** the dog's *drive* is more critical to training than labeling it. (But to help us understand each other better, definitions and explanations of terms in *italics* appear in the Glossary.)

Working in *drive* creates a clear, concentrated, confident dog, not at all hectic. *Drive* is purposeful and productive. *Drive* creates focus, action and animation.

High *drive* creates intense focus and fast action. But the work is done **calmly**. Be careful not to mistake *nervousness* or hectic action for *drive*.

Each *drive* has its own intensity factor, as well as its own limitations for each dog. The individual dog's *hardness*

(Terms appearing in *italics* are defined in the Glossary.)

3

affects his ability to remain in *drive*. Each dog's *energy level* and *condition* determine how he responds to training. His *stamina* dictates how much he wants to do at each session.

How the dog responds to training depends on other factors too. These include body sensitivity, physical ability, cooperation level, *emotional sensitivity*, past experiences and *nerve strength*. Our responsibility is to **read** each dog to make sure that what we are teaching is, in fact, what the dog is actually learning!

Who's Driving Who?

What you teach Champ (short for Champion, of course!) is how **he** can drive **you** to get what **he** wants. This makes Champ feel in control.

Dogs are good manipulators. It comes naturally to them. One barks in the kennel for attention. Another stares at the biscuit box, drooling. (Is there any doubt what he wants?) Yet another paws incessantly to be petted. Or he drops the ball in your lap repeatedly, driving you to throw it.

Dogs learn quickly how to get what **they** want. One of ours took only two sessions to learn to present her metal food dish to be fed. She's been pushing us daily now for five years!

Not just "stupid pet tricks," habits learned this way last longer than any compulsive training. They are more reliable, and certainly more **enjoyable** for the dog!

So to train Champ to perform with **Attention, Attitude** and **Accuracy**, all you do is find the proper *motivation*. Then you show him how to reach his *reward* – by doing what **you** want him to do, naturally.

4

Sound simple? It is **simple**. But it is not always **easy**.

The techniques explained here **are** simple. And they work – provided the dog himself has the necessary *drive*. But they take time. This cannot be a "quick fix."

Building the layers of **Foundation** for the eventual smooth road to success takes a long time. But the reward of a **happy** working dog is worth it, (not to mention making it fun for the handler)!

Obedience First

Obedience training is the basis for all three phases of the Schutzhund sport. While obedience may not be the first taught formally, eventual success springs only from optimum obedience.

The V-rated protection performance must present perfect obedience. The high-scoring tracking dog must use his nose the way **we** want him to, shunning his own instinctive air-scenting tendencies. And more and more often these days, judges insist on **Attitude** to score a V-rating in obedience.

The techniques herein teach you how to train through *drive* to create that all-important **Attitude**.

We divide each exercise into **Goal, Foundation** and **Polishing**.

This operator's manual teaches you how to work the drives. Just like the manual for your car teaches you how to shift gears, this one shows you how to shift your dog through *drive* into **overdrive**!

(Terms appearing in *italics* are defined in the Glossary.)

Our motto here at The Whatever Works School of Dog Training is – " Having **fun** now! "

Absorb and adhere to the general guidelines in the next few chapters. Read through the entire book first to get " the big picture. "

Then follow the step by step instructions for each exercise, from Getting Started to Putting It All Together.

Congratulations! You and Champ are on your way to becoming graduates of The Whatever Works (Best) School of Dog Training. But only if you and your dog are " **having fun now!** "

2. ATTITUDE.

Chapter 2

How?

The higher your structure is to be,
the deeper must be its foundation.
            – St. Augustine

Each exercise is divided into three training parts:

Goal + Foundation + Polishing.

The Goal is to produce a dog who works high in *drive* and channels all energy into correct performance.

Foundation work teaches the dog how to get what he wants through correct performance.

Polishing makes the dog work with even more concentration to reach his *reward* through precision and absolute control.

Setting a **Goal** for each exercise is extremely important. Know exactly how you want Champ to perform. Work toward that ideal. Keep a perfect picture in your mind.

Building the **Foundation** takes a long time. But it is the most important part of the training.

Final **Polishing** can begin only when the foundation is

complete and Champ is absolutely sure what you expect of him.

The first step is to create a correct *imprint* for each action. Champ's **first** impression of any activity forms a lifetime memory.

Your dog's brain is not a video machine. You cannot press " Rewind–Erase " and start over. A correct beginning is vital to future success.

Yes, dogs can be retrained. But when a dog gets stressed mentally (worried) or stressed physically (tired), he reverts to his **Foundation**, which includes his *imprint*.

That is the reason why the original behavior of retrained ("patchwork") dogs usually shows up on the trial field rather than in practice. In these cases, don't blame the repairman, blame the builder!

The best overall **Goal** is to make your dog the best he can be (or at least the best dog **you** can make him), and have fun while doing it! This allows for your dog's limitations, as well as your own capabilities. It may require compromise. Dispel thoughts of training your dog to please every judge.

Train for performance that satisfies **you**, meets your goals, and is rewarding because you and your dog both do your best. This helps make trials as much fun as training!

Motivation

Motivation is attracting Champ with what makes him **want** to work. Motivational training might take a little longer in the beginning, but it builds a much stronger **Foundation**.

Motivation steers the dog into the proper position. Through correct behavior, the dog then gets what **he** wants.

Once Champ learns this, he begins driving you (getting into the proper position with **Attention** and **Accuracy**) to get what **he** wants, instead of vice-versa (you trying to get him in the right position).

Create correct habits from the start. First comes constant *positive reinforcement,* then constant *reward.* **Foundation** is followed by variable and random *positive reinforcement,* but still constant *reward.*

Scientifically speaking, there is no difference between *positive reinforcement* and *reward.* In science, *positive reinforcement* is anything which is added to a behavior to increase its frequency or duration or intensity. Anything that occurs within a few seconds of that behavior is considered a possible reinforcer if it increases the behavior.

However, for our training purposes, it is helpful for us to differentiate between *positive reinforcement* and *reward.* Reinforcement comes **while** the dog is actually performing a certain behavior. *Reward* comes **after** the dog has completed the action correctly.

Thus steering a young dog into a sit by holding food over his head and letting him nibble at it **while** he sits correctly is *positive reinforcement.* Giving him the ball and releasing him **after** he sits is *reward.*

(Terms appearing in *italics* are defined in the Glossary.)

When teaching with *motivation*, each small step in the right direction is reinforced. The technical term is *shaping* behavior.

The psychology of *shaping* and *positive reinforcement* is explained in detail in <u>Don't Shoot the Dog</u> by dolphin trainer Karen Pryor. (See Chapter 2: Shaping: Developing Super Performance Without Strain or Pain.)

In *shaping*, you reinforce each move toward correct position. You respond to each attempt, in direct proportion to how great or small the effort. **Ask** for effort; don't **force** it.

Positive reinforcement or *reward* comes only for **Attention** with **Accuracy**. But it comes consistently, **every** time!

Lack of attention is not corrected for some time. Avoid trying to **make** your dog attentive. Simply resolve to make yourself the most interesting thing on the field to him!

When he does pay **Attention**, he gets what he wants. He does not get what he wants, however, just for having a good **Attitude** and having fun.

Motivational training is constructive. He gets what he wants only through **Attention** with **Accuracy**.

Knowing how to get what he wants improves Champ's **Attitude**. He thinks **he** is in control.

Champ **wants** to keep working. He keeps on trying. But he only gets what he wants when he is attentive and in the proper position.

Any disobedience is not reinforced, either positively or negatively. Unwanted behavior is simply ignored.

Corrections come only during or after the final **Polishing** phase. By then Champ clearly knows what you expect and how to avoid any future corrections. This makes any correction fair and constructive, not destructive.

Training Sessions

When using *motivation,* sessions are short. Training ends while Champ is at the **peak** of his *drive* and still wants more.

He comes to the next session a little more eager. That session ends again when he is a little higher in *drive,* thus creating even more enthusiasm and a better **Attitude** with each training session.

This only happens when work stops **before** the dog's *drive* diminishes. Avoid the " One-More-Time Syndrome. " Stop when Champ is at his best and still wants **more.**

Motivational training prevents " cadaver obedience. " (That's when the only way to tell the dog is not dead is that he's still moving!) " Cadaver obedience " is no fun to train, no fun to watch, and doesn't earn V-ratings!

Step By Step

Building the **Foundation** is done step by step. Missing a step in the beginning takes more time to fix later. Patchwork is never as good as a correct **Foundation** – built over time through motivational training.

(Terms appearing in *italics* are defined in the Glossary.)

Whenever training is not proceeding as it should, **back up** a step or two. End on success.

Start your next session at the previous successful level. Use *motivation* and begin with a training sequence that **does** work with your dog. When you move on again, the problem usually disappears.

Each step of the **Foundation** relies on the steps built before. When one step is not quite solid, it might still support one or two steps on top.

But finally one additional step collapses those below – all the way back down to the weakest step. That is why sometimes you must go back two or three steps, not just one.

In true motivational training, the dog often **does** the right thing **before** he understands it. Remember that Champ only really **learns** through many, many repetitions.

The first few times he gets it right, it is not because he really **knows** what to do. Reinforce the correct behavior over and over, making it a habit, before moving on to the next step. Create the correct habit and it lasts a lifetime.

Patchwork

When a dog has been trained incorrectly, or his **Foundation** training was done through compulsion, motivational work is **more** difficult and takes much longer. This dog may sit when told, but he does so without **Attention**, or slowly because of his poor **Attitude**, or without **Accuracy**.

Understand that training this dog takes more time, and is not always so successful. You can never create a proper *imprint* for the work. That first impression always remains.

Rebuilding a functional **Foundation** takes much longer, possibly twice as long as the previous training, if it can be done at all. And remember that stress (mental or physical) usually causes the dog to revert to his initial **Foundation**, no matter how effective your retraining may have been. (Again, blame the builder, not the repairman!)

Give this dog a fair chance. Keep working at building a better **Foundation**.

Be especially careful not to reinforce disobedience. The dog doesn't get what he wants **just** for having a good time, only for doing the job properly. Through repetition and rewarding every success, this dog may learn to enjoy training more and improve his **Attitude**.

Realize that this patchwork may have to be done through force training after all. Sometimes the only way to fix training done through **incorrect** use of force, is with the **correct** use of force. You may eventually have to sacrifice some **Attitude** for **Accuracy**.

Evaluate Your Dog

Whether your dog is young and just starting, or in need of retraining, be honest in your evaluation. Set realistic goals for performance.

Drives **can** be built (if they are present), but you need to recognize just where you are starting. As you work with your dog, honestly assess his components. Determine how much compromise may be necessary.

___

(Terms appearing in *italics* are defined in the Glossary.)

Consider his physical abilities and any limitations. Be aware of his inherent body sensitivity, *emotional sensitivity*, cooperation level and *nerve strength*, as well as any past experiences and training.

Many consider the German Shepherd Dog the ideal working partner. But some dogs could benefit from a bit o' the Belgian (energy and sensitivity), a bit o' the Golden (object obsession and retrieving drive), or sometimes even a bit o' the husky (*hardness*)!

Having the right combination enhances the character and trainability of the **ideal** dog. But being realistic about the dog you are working is the key to better training.

Evaluate Yourself

While much depends on what your dog has to offer, how far he goes definitely depends on what **you** bring to the training sessions. How you motivate him and apply the techniques show in his performance. Your physical capabilities, temperament, timing, understanding and ability to read your dog all determine the success of your training.

Being realistic about your own potential is best. Whatever your aspirations and limitations, correct training requires patience, consistency and discipline.

You cannot be lazy. You **must** put in the time to get the results.

This is a sport. Come to each training session ready to **play** the game.

Be a good sport with your dog. Remember he is your teammate. You are not here to trick him, but to learn to work together.

Keep negative emotions out of training. Dogs are emotional creatures. Many are extremely sensitive to the mood and demeanor of pack members – especially you, the leader.

This trait of cooperation is often pronounced in many of our true working dogs. Your bringing the right **Attitude** to training goes a long way to inspire Champ.

If you have difficulty applying these techniques effectively, work with an experienced trainer familiar with what you are doing. Watching others, and having them watch and guide you, are valuable learning tools.

That's one reason we have clubs for Schutzhund! Some work cannot be done alone.

If your own negative attitude affects your training, work around another person. Most of us avoid losing our temper in front of others. Try playing calming music.

If the opposite is true (people make you more nervous), work alone until you are confident in the techniques and Champ is responding nicely. Find what works **best** for you and Champ and use it.

Stay cool and calm no matter what happens. Relax! Avoid being in a hurry.

Learn to take deep breaths. Laugh and smile while training. Enjoy your training time with your dog! Remember, we are supposed to be " having **fun** now! "

(Terms appearing in *italics* are defined in the Glossary.)

Tone of Voice

Give commands in a light, soft voice with a pleasant tone. Champ has keen hearing.

You get more **Attention** with a whisper than a shout. Save the volume for when you really need it.

Tone of voice is often more important than what you say. This is especially true in the motion exercises (sit, down and stands).

Practice your commands (off the field) consistently in the right tone until they become a habit. The stress of a trial tends to change your tone of voice, so *imprint* yourself correctly, the same as you do your dog.

Make proper commands a habit, so you get them **right** when it counts. We practice tone of voice for certain commands while driving (in the privacy of the car), as well as whenever we walk through the routine without our dogs (which we do frequently.)

Body Language

As important as your attitude and tone of voice is body language. Natural communication for dogs is body language, not words. Commands are often secondary to body cues for your dog.

Champ keys on even slight body movements (whether intentional or not), long before he learns the **verbal** commands. Even your breathing is extremely relevant to Champ.

An *anthropomorphic* owner thinks his dog is sad and compassionate because he shows great interest when the owner is crying. In truth, dogs react to even slight variances in breathing patterns – and crying creates a **major** difference in breathing.

Champ notices slight changes in your breathing, as well as even minor body movements. So when you get stressed or nervous in a trial, and your breathing becomes rapid and shallow, he senses that.

Most people start to fidget, too. Taking a slow, deep breath before the start of each exercise helps get the body signals back to normal (even if you've still got butterflies in your stomach)!

So be aware of both your breathing and body movement in your training and handling. Then you'll be able to help Champ come trial day.

Opposition Reflex

Another essential element of your dog's nature is his *opposition reflex*. When you pull or hold your dog, he automatically leans **against** the pressure.

We activate this reflex in protection work when we hold the dog **back.** This creates tension going **forward.**

This also shows with the young puppy on the leash for the first time. The pup's reaction is always to pull **against** the pressure. Remember this picture.

This reflex is sometimes difficult for us to understand, probably because we do not possess the same physical

---

(Terms appearing in *italics* are defined in the Glossary.)

capability as our dogs. If we pull hard on something that releases suddenly, we fall back.

This does not happen to the adult dog. His opposite muscles automatically take over, usually quickly enough to prevent him from losing any ground.

Be acutely aware of this reflex in training. A tight leash almost always creates **opposite** tension.

Remember all those dogs in Beginner Obedience Class dragging their owners around while the instructor bellowed, " Loose leash! Loose leash! " ? The teacher was just trying to break that *opposition reflex* !

If you want your dog to stand solidly and not move forward, holding him back is the **least** likely route to success. More about that later. Keep the *opposition reflex* in mind and use it to your advantage in training.

Dogs can exhibit an *opposition reflex* in their **Attitude** too. (Some would call this dog stubborn.)

When the handler wants the dog to do something, the dog immediately resents the control. Just as we tend to fall back when what we are pulling breaks loose, this emotional pressure has a way of backfiring on us with our dogs too.

So it is easier to teach the dog how **he** can be in control. He's more willing when he's driving **you** to get what he wants, instead of vice-versa.

Petting vs. Praising

There is a world of difference between petting and praising. Using both effectively requires you to know the difference.

Praise is **verbal** and petting is **physical**. Praise comes with *positive reinforcement* or *reward*. Champ doesn't get his usual *reward* during a trial, so you want him to understand praise.

Praise indicates that *reward* is imminent. Condition Champ what to expect. Then praise makes him **more** attentive to you.

There are two kinds of praise – calm reassurance and cheerleading. Here again, **tone** is more important than **what** you say. But be consistent in your words, as well as your tone, to help Champ learn.

Energetic dogs need calm praise. Unsure dogs also need calm praise.

Lethargic dogs need cheerleading. These dogs need **you** to get excited before they do.

Praise can be encouraging or it can be energizing. Different kinds are used at various points in training, depending on the desired result and the dog's *temperament*.

Praise is something your dog is supposed to **like** and want to work for. So be sure you are on **his** wave length.

Try this experiment. Wait until your dog is just hanging out in the house or yard and is not too distracted.

Without using his name, offer verbal praise the same way you do in training – same words and tone of voice. If he does not look at you immediately and at least wag his tail with enthusiasm, your praise is not effective. It is not meaningful to **him**.

(Terms appearing in *italics* are defined in the Glossary.)

Real praise elicits **Attention** with positive expectation. He should expect to be petted, at the very least. Truly effective praise makes him look to you eagerly, anticipating something good is about to happen.

Learn to communicate with Champ. Praise in a way that is meaningful to **him.**

Praise and petting do not always go together in training. But Champ must be conditioned to accept both.

When he downs quickly on command after that flying voraus, you **want** to be able to praise him (even though you cannot pet him or *reward* him right away.) But you **don't want** him to jump up and break position or lose concentration.

Through consistency in training, you teach Champ to accept both praise and petting individually, without becoming distracted by them or relying on them. So pay attention to whether the techniques call for praise or petting and for what reason.

As with praise, there are also two kinds of petting. Smooth stroking along the dog's shoulders and back **calms** and reassures the dog, giving him confidence.

Patting the ribs vigorously creates **energy**, excitement and enthusiasm. Like praise, each type has its place at certain moments in training.

In the basic position (sit), pet Champ under his chin or behind his ears, not on top of the head or muzzle. Most dogs don't like us reaching over their head and we want petting to be pleasant, and thus productive.

Make praise and petting count. Be careful not to overdo either.

Constant praise dulls the dog to your voice and makes it meaningless. Inappropriate or continual petting also destroys its meaning to the dog.

Exuberant praise can make a dog too crazy to concentrate. If the recipe calls for a pinch, a pound is not always better.

Petting at the wrong time distracts the dog instead of helping him. Use both appropriately and make both meaningful.

For those working an imported dog – praise in English, not German. Praise must come from the heart.

Sincerity can get lost in translation. What is most spontaneous for you works best. Your dog will understand!

<u>Release</u>

Each exercise must have a clear **beginning** and a clear **ending**. The dog understands best if training is black and white, with no grey areas. A dog gets worried wondering whether he is supposed to be doing something, but not knowing what.

Teach Champ right away to work in **Attention** from the initial command until a clear release. The time from command to release lengthens as his attention span and understanding progress. The release is always clear, and not to be confused with praise or petting.

(Terms appearing in *italics* are defined in the Glossary.)

Develop an **explosive** release. Ideally, the dog leaps in the air full of joy at being released. Keep in mind that Champ will eventually work in a trial just for the release. Develop a release that your dog likes – motivational and full of energy.

Many handlers use Okay! as a release word. This is a poor choice, though, because it is a common (and often unconscious) part of speech.

Free! or Ya! work better. But your release command must be the same every time. Use the word as you throw your hands up in the air. Invite your dog to jump up. You can use a toy or food in your hand at first to get him to jump with energy.

Avoid reaching down to your dog and keep your hands out of his face and eyes. Most dogs dislike this and find it annoying. Raise your arms to encourage him to jump and focus **upward**. In most cases, move him in the direction of the exercise for the release.

Praise is not a release! Be sure to avoid using any sort of praise word for your release command.

Remember, you want Champ to **remain** in position while you praise him. Releasing with praise confuses your dog and creates a large grey area. He thinks praise might mean release.

Keep the two clearly separate. Your special command, plus raising your arms and moving quickly out of position, all make the release different from petting or praising.

Always **play** or romp with Champ for the first few seconds after his release. He then becomes more focused within the exercise and begins to work **for** the release.

The way a dog reacts to the release tells you a great

deal about his *temperament* and what sort of praise he needs. If he leaps to your chest or bites at your face, you probably want to keep your praise **calm** during training.

If you get just a few steps and a wagging tail, you can get a little more **excited** with your praise. This dog needs some cheerleading!

But be sure not to confuse release with praise or petting. Praise is constructive and comes when Champ is doing something correctly, **while** he is still concentrating within the exercise. Petting also has a specific function within an exercise – to encourage or reassure, or even distract.

Neither praise nor petting comes after a release. Being released takes no great talent, effort or concentration. Praise and petting must both be earned.

After release comes **play**, not praise or petting. Keep these three (release, praise and petting) clearly separate and your training becomes more constructive.

Approach each training session with the right attitude. Know **exactly** what you want to work on.

There might not be any overnight miracles. Using these methods can take longer than correction-based training. But it lasts longer, looks better and is way more **fun**!

Remember, you get back only what you put in. Give Champ 100 percent of your **Attention** if you expect all of his. He gives you 100 percent concentration and effort **only** if you first give him the same.

(Terms appearing in *italics* are defined in the Glossary.)

3. ACTIVATING DRIVE.

Chapter 3

Drives

*Dogs have a lot to communicate
to a person who's willing to listen.*
— Susan Butcher

We work with five basic drives. (These definitions are for our purposes in training, not from academic ethology.)

Food drive is the dog's desire to persist in getting food – not always related to hunger.

Play drive is the dog's obsession with objects and his desire to entertain himself actively.
Prey drive is the dog's intensity in chasing anything moving away – catching, biting and carrying it.

Fight drive is the dog's desire to initiate and persist in confrontation, both physical and mental.
Pack drive is the dog's desire to work with the handler and be a member of the team.

Training in *drive* has two requirements:
·The dog must **have** the *drive* to do the work.
·You must understand **how** to activate the *drive*.

Every dog possesses certain drives, but each to a different degree. *Drive* can often be built, but you can rarely instill it where it is not present.

A draft horse cannot be made into a winning race horse, no matter how good the training.

We only have the **right** to work those dogs who have some natural inclination for the training. We do not have the right to try to train a dog beyond his capabilities.

The dog has a right to **enjoy** his work. We should not continue training when the dog has no joy in his work. With some dogs, it is only right to stop at basic obedience and not attempt to make them competition dogs.

For those dogs who **do** have the *drive*, however, we owe it to them to find the best way to train them. So we must discover the proper *motivation*.

The combination of drives in each dog is his personal telephone number. There are only so many numerals (drives). But every dog has a little different combination in a different order (degree). Unfortunately for us, they don't come with a phone book!

The *motivation* is the phone number you use to reach each dog. To communicate with him, push the right buttons to activate his drives. Find the right combination of buttons and you **reach** the dog.

Through watching and reading Champ, you find out what motivates him. You discover what makes him respond. Then channel that *drive*, through *motivation*, into the desired behavior or action.

Which Drive?

The most important decision is **which** *drive* to use when. The obvious answer is to use the dog's strongest *drive*. This is not always the case, however.

A dog with an overwhelming *food drive* can become so crazed with getting the food that it actually inhibits learning if *reward* does not come soon enough. Here you must make the *drive* concentrated and focused by responding to Champ the first instant he is correct.

Likewise, a dog with strong *fight drive* can get obsessed with winning the fight and lose the calmness needed to concentrate. Enthusiastic dogs can get overloaded in *play drive* and forget correct position when you do not respond quickly enough.

Learning occurs when the dog is calm and concentrated. Any of the drives can inhibit learning if they stress Champ or make him frantic. Watch out for this in the beginning phases of training.

Different drives work best for certain exercises. And there is a countless variety of options for combining the drives in any exercise and training session.

However, consistency within the program is important. The sooner Champ knows what to **expect**, the faster learning proceeds.

Watch Champ constantly during the first steps in each exercise. He shows you the best way to keep his **Attention.**

(Terms appearing in *italics* are defined in the Glossary.)   27

Subtle signs tell you he is losing focus. That is the moment to reinforce, **before** he loses interest.

Persist with using the *motivation*, even if it doesn't work instantly. This is a new game to Champ and he needs time to **learn** how to play. Resolve to succeed, not just try.

Be persistent, as well as consistent, until he knows what to expect. If his *drive* does not increase as he learns the game plan, however, try pushing a different button and working in another *drive*. Use new *motivation*.

Food Drive

The *motivation* for *food drive* is hot dogs. Slice them into pieces the size of a nickel. Or leave the hot dog whole for the dog to nibble if this works better. Cheese can be motivating, but is more perishable (and so mushy).

The greatest advantage to using food is that you can reinforce while Champ is still in the correct position. With the sit, for example, you can feed Champ **while** he sits correctly, not **after**.

And you can *reward* without having him break position. With play, prey, or fight, the dog must move out of position somewhat when he gets what he wants.

Food is usually the most effective way to steer Champ into the right position. Simply withhold the food (by closing your hand around it) until he gets into correct position, then feed immediately.

Food drive is also one of the easiest to build. When you reduce his normal ration, he becomes more eager to work for food.

Substitute a small amount of food with a vitamin supplement at mealtime, rather than no food at all, especially with a young dog. Experiment with different types of food if hot dogs just don't interest him. (String cheese comes neatly packaged for slicing.)

There are those "chow hounds," however, for whom food is not related to hunger. It is an obsession.

These try to eat your entire hand when they realize it might contain food. A finger or a hot dog – it's all the same to them.

Away from the training field, even at home, first teach this dog to be more careful. Start **after** the dog has been fed.

Withhold the slice of hot dog (by closing your fingers) until he takes it properly and gently without snapping or biting hard. As you tell him Easy or Gently, you may have to tap the **front** of his nose (not the top – it's too delicate) a few times to make your point.

Don't worry, a few such raps won't extinguish this dog's *food drive*. Instead, he becomes more focused and determined to get what he wants so badly.

Usually slices work best for these dogs, rather than letting them nibble the end of a whole wiener. (One chow hound actually grabbed and swallowed an entire hot dog from the trainer's hand in one snatch!) As a last resort, you can wear protective gloves such as those made for fish scaling or butchering.

Keep in mind that with such a dog, food can inhibit learning and work against your training goals. Keep your dog calm and reinforce only **Accuracy**, but do it immediately.

(Terms appearing in *italics* are defined in the Glossary.)

You don't want to use food? You think it's bribery? You think the dog should work **just** for you (*pack drive*)?

Would you be happier going to work each day just to please your boss? Or your mate? Or would you rather receive something you like, such as money? Would you do a better job and have a better attitude if you went to work just because someone would hurt you if you didn't?

Even a workaholic strives harder when he gets what he wants out of it. We all work better for *reward* rather than just to avoid the consequences. Dogs do too!

We enjoy work more when we are shown what to do **before** we get pushed around or coerced. Working strictly in *pack drive* requires correction first (to get the dog in the right position), before praise.

Only *anthropomorphic* owners believe that dogs trained by such methods really work only for them. These dogs work either purely in *pack drive* or simply to avoid the compulsion. Such work can produce **Attention** and **Accuracy**, but rarely a dynamite **Attitude**.

Play Drive

Play is incorporated into each training session. But this play is constructive. Champ's **Attitude** gets better each session because he knows he is going to have fun!

Note that the play is **within** the training session. When play comes **after** training, your dog only learns that playing is more fun than training. Play must be part of the training, not separate.

Play includes elements of prey, retrieving and sometimes fighting. The difficulty with using play a lot in actual training is that the dog must be in excellent *condition*, with lots of *stamina*. Also, the handler must be endowed with precise coordination and superb timing to use play constructively.

The *motivation* for *play drive* is two pieces of hose – 8 to 10 inches long and one to two inches in diameter. Lengths of garden hose work, but heavy rubber automotive heater hose lasts longer and dogs enjoy biting down on it. (The hot water hose even comes in red so you can find it in the grass!)
Or you can make (or buy) rolls of burlap the same size. This is a perfect use for those worn out sleeve covers you've been saving. Use non-toxic glue on one side and roll **tightly**.

Hoses or burlap rolls are better than balls because they don't bounce. Many a dog has been seriously injured after leaping into the air for a ball.

Dogs' bodies are strong and resilient when traveling in a straight line. But their anatomy was not designed to withstand the impact of landing in a twisted position. (This is also why landing from catching a Frisbee has crippled many dogs.)
The winner of the 1990 DVG Deutsche Meister in Germany, a talented and agile Belgian Malinois named Igor, was laid up for months with a shattered bone in his hock from catching a single throw of an errant tennis ball that bounced the wrong way. Sadly, the higher the dog's **desire** for the ball, the more prone he is to injury playing this dangerous game.

(Terms appearing in *italics* are defined in the Glossary.)   31

4. EXCITE DOG AND THROW FIRST HOSE.

5. AS SOON AS THE DOG DROPS
ONE HOSE, YOU THROW THE OTHER ONE.

The colored dye on a tennis ball is toxic. The fuzzy outer surface is abrasive and wears down the enamel on the dog's teeth, leading to cracked, chipped and broken teeth.

Pieces of chewed up tennis balls have caused serious medical emergencies, including intestinal impactions that require surgery. So please, save your tennis balls for the courts and your Frisbees for the beach!

Besides, hoses are cheaper and more versatile. You can gradually make them smaller and smaller so they are easy to conceal as training progresses.

You can play tug-of-war and incite *fight drive* with a hose. This is difficult with a ball.

Sticks can be used occasionally, but only if nothing else is available. A dog who strikes quickly for the stick can injure himself. Once you've seen a dog poke himself in the eye or bloody his mouth from running into the end of a stick, you'll prefer the soft hoses.

The hose lands solidly in one place, so the dog gets more intense in striking quickly and snatching the hose from the ground. This creates good basics for the retrieve.

Teach Champ to play with **two** hoses. Whatever you use, both objects must be identical.

Tease him until he really wants the hoses. (See Fig. 3, Page 24.) Show him that you have two hoses (Fig. 4).

Throw the first hose **just a few feet** to one side. Just as Champ picks it up, call his name and show him you have the second hose. If he doesn't react right away, wave and wiggle it. Make it come alive!

Assume a body posture that shows you're going to throw the second hose (Fig. 5). Then attract him with it until he wants it. (Here you are using the hose as *motivation* to incite Champ's *play drive*.)

The **moment** Champ drops the first hose, toss the second several feet to your other side so Champ has to cross **in front** of you to get to it (Fig. 5). After he crosses in front, you run to where he dropped the first hose.

As Champ picks up the second hose, call his name and get his attention with the first hose again. Assume the throwing posture and, as soon as he drops his hose, the sequence starts again (Fig. 5).

Aim at getting Champ to cross **in front** of you on his way to get the other hose (Fig. 5). The game eventually has Champ running in a straight line with you in the middle.

The **Goal** is to get him to run back to you and, just as he gets near you, show him the second hose so he drops the first one close to you. You then **immediately** throw the second hose so Champ keeps moving in a straight line (Fig. 5).

This playing makes **you** the center of the game. It reinforces the center line, which we use continually in training. Playing with two hoses eliminates the " keep-away" game many dogs become so fond of playing.

Besides building a strong positive *imprint* for retrieving, it motivates Champ to come back with his prize as fast as he went out. This is an important element of training the retrieve. The hoses also become the basic *motivation* for the recall and voraus when incorporated into the training program, and the two-hose game becomes the *reward*.

Another major benefit of this type of play is that it develops physical *condition*. Champ builds the muscles needed for the fast take-off, quick sprint, the strike and quick pivot turn. Playing with two hoses during each training session builds *stamina* and endurance.

As Champ learns the game and builds *condition*, he gets faster. Speed makes a dog feel free.

Speed is a great energizer and stress reliever. Like driving a car fast, speed also increases concentration.

When first teaching the two-hose game, your dog will probably come up with some creative variations. He might not pick up the first hose if he knows you have another one.

He might keep the first and try to get the second one from you too. He might run right past you with the first hose without dropping it.

This is your first opportunity to read Champ and start channeling his *drive* into the behavior you want (without shouting commands and jerking his neck). Throw the second hose **only** when he drops the first, but throw it **instantly**.

Through your immediate reaction, Champ starts to understand how to get what he wants. This game is the ideal start for you and Champ to work together and develop your timing.

Two hoses is the **only** game you play with Champ now. All his *play drive* must be channeled with **you** at the center.

By throwing a single stick or a ball at other times, you miss an excellent opportunity. You also invite incorrect

---

(Terms appearing in *italics* are defined in the Glossary.)   35

behavior (returning to you slowly or playing " keep-away").

You know you are on the right track when Champ picks up whatever you throw and **flies** back to you looking for the second one. Even our most ball-crazy dogs now opt for the two-hose game, even when there's a ball around!

Now is the time to start building Champ's vocabulary. Just as he drops the hose, tell him Out.

If he doesn't drop the hose, don't tell him again or go after him. Just make the one you have come alive.

When he finally does drop his hose, just say Out, Good Dog, and **instantly** throw the other hose. He'll soon get the word association and learn how to make this fun game continue.

When Champ is excited about the hoses and knows the two-hose game, teach him the command Get It. Allow him to jump up and grab one hose while you hold it. (Watch your hand!) Then play tug-of-war with Champ and let him win.

To use the hose as *motivation* within training, you must teach Champ to focus on the hose, but not grab for it until you say Get It. Lengthen the time into several seconds he must wait and watch the hose before being allowed to Get It. This builds focus and concentration through *drive*.

Use the second hose to get Champ back right away after he wins. Avoid allowing him to go off and chew on the hose or play by himself. This game comes **only** from you and you are always the center.

At the end of play, always tease Champ with one or both hoses before putting them away (unless he's already **crazy** for them). This builds his desire for the next session.

Building Drive

With a dog who isn't excited about the hoses, you need to build *drive*. This requires teasing the dog and **not** letting him get it.

Start by tying him up. If you have another dog who plays with the hoses, let the reluctant dog watch to create interest.

Or you can play with the hoses yourself. You have to be a good actor here and really make the dog believe you are having a grand time!

Move closer and closer until you are tossing the hose right in front of him but he still can't get it. This is to build *drive*, so there is no relief until he shows real enthusiasm and desire to grab the hose.

When your dog **does** get excited, let him grab the hose once. Then steal it away. Tease him again and end the session.

Remember to stop while he is still high in *drive*. Repeat similar sessions until your dog really wants to play the minute he sees the hoses.

Once he's showing strong interest, take him off the line and toss the hose back and forth with a friend, having your dog be "monkey-in-the-middle." Continue to build his enthusiasm until you see that this is a game he really wants to play.

Here again is an opportunity to read your dog – to figure out how to motivate him and see when he's ready to move on. Find out what works!

(Terms appearing in *italics* are defined in the Glossary.)

Puppy Imprinting

Even young puppies can be introduced to the basics of playing with two hoses. But remember, they can last only about three tosses.

Puppies soon begin to lose concentration, as well as physical ability. Any activity with a puppy or young dog must be extremely short because it must end **before** *drive* diminishes.

Puppies can be **introduced** to certain activities, but they cannot actually **learn** them yet. Stop as soon as they start to get the idea. Avoid letting them tire of this game! Keep it fun.

Without coordination and concentration, they cannot bring the full physical power and mental intensity we want to the exercises. Make a good *imprint,* but stop before you create bad habits.

Prey Drive

The chase factor is important to recognize. Many dogs have *prey drive* that can be developed into play.

Many young dogs chase an object when it is moving away. Chasing, pouncing, biting, shaking and carrying are all elements of prey behavior.

While some dogs bite and carry the prey object instantly when they catch it, some don't. Some don't even show enough *drive* to initiate the chase.

Such a dog needs help to develop a workable *play drive.* Constructive teasing (as outlined previously in Building Drive) often results in a dog who learns to play.

Evaluation of the **desire** to chase is instrumental in choosing a candidate for this sport. A strong *prey drive* enhances training in the protection phase.

It is important to make a clear distinction between *prey drive* and play. They are related, but they are not the same.

If you are starting with a dog who shows no *drive* for chasing or playing, have someone experienced help you evaluate this dog. Training a dog who has no inclination for the work is a thankless job for the handler and unfair to the dog.

Fight Drive

The desire to fight often can be seen even in very young puppies. This one loves tug-of-war and, even when he wins, comes right back for more.

Such dogs often look for confrontation. Some bite and pull at stationary objects, creating the fight themselves.

For a dog who enjoys this fight, it can be channeled and used as meaningful *motivation* for certain exercises. Start by playing tug-of-war with the hoses, but teach this dog to wait before allowing him to Get It (as explained before).

This *drive* is used later in training, in the retrieve and for **Polishing** some of the other exercises. But be careful when activating *fight drive* too early.

While still building the **Foundation**, we encourage the dog to drive the handler to get what he wants. Here Champ comes to believe he is in control, however, so fighting can get out of hand.

Using *fight drive* in foundation training can be counterproductive, and even dangerous with some dogs. So save it for later.

Once the handler assumes complete control, the *fight drive* can then be used to heighten intensity. When the dog shows strong desire to fight, leave it alone until **after** the handler has clearly established who's in charge.

Pack Drive

Dominance and submission are the essential elements of the pack. Dogs are pack animals. How each dog functions within the structure and how he perceives human pack members varies.

For our purposes, *pack drive* is not the same as dominance. *Pack drive* is the dog's desire to work **within** the framework of the pack, whether the role be dominant or subordinate.

All compulsion relies on *pack drive*. This *drive* greatly influences how each dog responds to pressure from the handler. Corrections can create avoidance in a dog with low *pack drive*.

In our format, initial training relies heavily on *motivation* through the other drives. Working solely in *pack drive* is usually the opposite of real motivational training.

It is true, though, that the bond with his handler can be motivational for the dog. With a willing, cooperative dog, he enjoys working for praise and petting and the joy of being part of the team. This dog has high *pack drive*.

Traditional obedience training insists that the handler continually reinforce his position as pack leader. Motivational training allows the dog to work for what **he** wants. In many ways, the dog perceives that he can control the situation.

After this strong *imprint* and **Foundation,** corrections may be introduced in **Polishing.** But corrections come only when the dog knows exactly what you expect.

For dogs high in *pack drive* and willing to cooperate for the good of the team, serious or frequent corrections are rarely necessary. When the dog enjoys working within the pack, even the fine-tuning for a perfect performance relies on very few corrections.

To learn to work with the drives and push the right buttons, watch Champ's reaction to every step of training. First identify and build his drives.

Find the right *motivation* to make him calm and concentrated. Reinforce each correct response. Perfect your timing.

Allow Champ to drive you to get what he wants through correct behavior – **Attention** and **Accuracy.** Improve his **Attitude** by heightening his *drive.*

(Terms appearing in *italics* are defined in the Glossary.)

6. PRONG COLLAR PROPERLY FITTED.

Chapter 4

Corrections

Animals suffer as much as we do.
– Albert Schweitzer

*Good training needs a kind heart
as well as a cool and well-informed head
for the proper application of necessary compulsion.*
– Konrad Most

Once you build a strong **Foundation** using Champ's drives, **Polishing** performance may require corrections to achieve your **Goal**. Before moving to this phase, however, honestly evaluate your teamwork with Champ.

He should have an excellent **Attitude** during training. From command to release, he should show intense **Attention** and perform with precise **Accuracy**.

Achieving this proper motivational **Foundation** usually takes about six months, working several times each week.

Without this solid **Foundation**, corrections can break the dog down. Performance deteriorates when it should start to sparkle. Be sure Champ is consistent and clear in his motivational work before introducing any corrections.

If you have been reinforcing and rewarding incorrect heel position, for example, and now you correct that behavior, it makes your dog confused and anxious.

Accuracy and **Attention** must be built through *motivation*. Otherwise, corrections just destroy **Attitude.**

Evaluate Champ's nature. Review his *temperament* and training before proceeding.

His body sensitivity determines how strong a correction he needs. His *emotional sensitivity* controls his perception of corrections from you.

His *nerve strength* provides his confidence – his sense of himself and reaction to correction. His *hardness* (within each *drive*) determines his ability to bounce back after correction and the degree to which any correction affects that *drive.*

Evaluate your own capability too. Timing is the **most** important element of any correction.

Are your reactions fast enough? Can you correct **without** negative emotion?

Have you developed consistently good habits in your commands, tone of voice and body posture? Is your relationship with Champ one of teamwork and trust?

Mistake vs. Disobedience

Corrections come only for **disobedience**, not for **mistakes.** Be sure Champ knows exactly what he is to do and how to get his *reward* in the exercise before introducing any sort of correction.

Thus, if Champ's entire foundation reinforced attention in heeling, then looking away is now a **disobedience.** A correction the instant he looks away brings him back in attention. You then provide *positive reinforcement* immediately.

At first though, simply being distracted is a **mistake**, not a **disobedience**. During foundation work, avoid allowing your dog to get distracted by building *drive* and adding more *motivation*.

Then during the **Polishing** stage, when we are sure that Champ knows what to do, correct for lack of **Attention**. But correction comes only when being distracted is a clear **disobedience**, not when it stems from low *drive*.

Standing for the sit in motion, however, is almost always a **mistake**. Missing a motion exercise is rarely **disobedience**.

Your dog does not think to himself that, although you told him to sit, he would prefer to stand. The cause here can be inconsistent handling, incorrect tone of voice, lack of proper foundation for the moving sit, or a learning plateau where the difference between the two commands simply is not clear to the dog right now.

A correction for a missed sit in motion produces anxiety and confusion because the dog does not know **how** to avoid the force. Best to go back to the basics before adding any corrections.

Positive reinforcement and then *reward*, with light commands and consistent handling, creates better performance here. Delay any correction for motion exercises until Champ is a seasoned veteran.

(Terms appearing in *italics* are defined in the Glossary.)　　45

Timing

The key element of a correction is **surprise**, not pain. Force is very short and instantly effective. A correction must have a shock value, and it must be absolute.

Any correction must be given with calm acceptance. It is followed **first** by *positive reinforcement* or *reward*. This is sometimes combined with reassuring praise and/or petting, when your dog's behavior is correct.

This teaches Champ to react to correction by channeling his *drive* with more intensity to get what he wants. He learns *reward* always follows correction, so he works harder to get it.

How a dog accepts a correction is influenced by his *pack drive*. In the pack, discipline is clear and sharp.

A mother's rebuke of an unruly pup is immediate. But the incident is over the moment the pup's behavior is acceptable.

Then they return to normal pack behavior. Ostracism is **never** part of pack discipline. Nor is nagging.

Nagging corrections go against a dog's nature. Pack discipline often seems violent, but it is effective the **first** time and makes a strong impression on the receiver.

Constant corrections are as detrimental to the dog as a handler's display of negative emotion. Both are destructive.

So correct timing is **essential**. A correction one second too late in heeling, for example, can come as Champ is looking back to you, not while he is looking away. This can do great damage.

Any sort of *punishment* for correct behavior is the fastest way to break down training. Correcting a **mistake**, rather than a true **disobedience**, creates confusion and quickly destroys the dog's confidence.

Be sure a correction is justified. Be sure it comes at the right instant. And be sure you remain **completely calm**.

Back in Drive

Correct **only** while Champ is in *drive*. If he is inattentive because his *drive* is low, excite him and motivate him more in training.

Build a stronger **Foundation**. Raise his *drive* within the exercise before introducing any correction.

After a correction, the **moment** he is right, motivate and get him back in *drive*. The training sequence is:

Drive – Force – Drive.

Always put Champ back in *drive* as quickly as possible after a correction.

Remember, when a dog is stressed he tends to revert to foundation training. Before you correct, build a strong motivational foundation.

An effective correction stresses the dog somewhat. But then he quickly comes back into *drive* for *motivation*, because this was his **Foundation**.

(Terms appearing in *italics* are defined in the Glossary.)

Sometimes, however, a correction stresses the dog enough that he comes entirely out of *drive*. A correction can inhibit *food drive* or *play drive* when these drives are lower.

This dog may refuse food or lose enthusiasm for playing following a correction. Continue offering the *motivation* used in foundation training, even if he is not interested. His *drive* comes back if his **Foundation** was thorough and correct.

Avoid correcting a dog who is unsure or worried. Motivate first. Avoid corrections until the dog is back in *drive* and showing confidence, not stress!

Some dogs consistently show avoidance after a correction and shut down for some time. These dogs generally have low *pack drive*. (Remember, *pack drive* for our purposes is the dog's desire to work **with** the handler, not just dominance.)

You need to work harder with these dogs to bring them back through *motivation*. What works depends on the level of their other drives and the strength of their **Foundation.**

Some dogs show aggression toward the handler after a correction. Such dogs are usually dominant, with high *fight drive*. Channel that *drive* back into the desired behavior through the *motivation* used in foundation training.

When an initial correction incites aggression (growling or snapping), this behavior can be merely a reaction to the situation and not an intentional challenge to the handler. Correcting the aggressive reaction here is unnecessary.

To the dog, he may be reacting to the surprise, not

necessarily challenging you. Avoid letting him push **your** emotional buttons.

Avoid going to war over behavior **you** caused. You only create another problem instead of solving this one.

Simply ignore any such unwanted behavior caused by a correction. Stay calm and show no emotion.

Continue working on the exercise. The aggressive behavior usually disappears quickly, especially when the dog learns to channel his *drive* into getting his *reward.*

With dogs who consistently show either avoidance or aggression after correction, and do not overcome it after one or two sessions, consult an experienced trainer familiar with these techniques. Both types can be difficult dogs to work and you may need help in reading the dog correctly to find the appropriate solution.

Effectiveness

Avoid force when the dog needs reassurance. If there is any question whether the behavior is definite **disobedience**, use the " Show and Tell" method first.

" Show" Champ what you want using *motivation,* and then " Tell" him he's a Good Dog when he's correct. Save the correction for when you are sure it's not just a **mistake**.

Stress from a previous correction sometimes causes a dog to make a mistake. Avoid using force for behavior produced by a previous correction.

If you correct inattention during heeling, for example,

---

and the next sit is slow and tense, motivate and then use *positive reinforcement.*

Help Champ be correct, and then *reward.* More corrections only create more confusion.

Also avoid correcting a second time in the same part of the pattern. The dog may lag or hesitate at the place where he was previously corrected.

Dogs first connect a correction with a particular location (*place association*). A second correction here only confirms their erroneous belief that the place caused the correction rather than the behavior. This delays understanding and inhibits learning.

Avoid correcting twice for the same disobedience, especially in the same place. The **first** correction makes the impression.

If it does not, then it was not effective. The timing was off, or **Foundation** work was insufficient so the dog does not know what you want or how to avoid the correction.

Your effectiveness, however, may not be apparent until **after** the next few repetitions of the exercise. The results of training, and what Champ is learning, are often not seen until the next session.

For example, correcting a wide about turn often creates anxiety for the next about turn. Motivate and *reward* the next few turns.

If the correction was effective, he usually gets it right the third or fourth time (probably in your next session). By then the stress of the correction is forgotten, but its purpose is not.

If the specific behavior does not improve after correction, determine why. Was **Foundation** training correct? Is correction timely? Are you overcorrecting or undercorrecting?

Is your dog stressed or confident? Are you getting emotional? Are you unknowingly warning before the correction? Consider these answers before deciding whether to correct again or cement the **Foundation.**

Correcting several times for the same disobedience means something is wrong. Either your timing is off, the correction is too harsh, there is no surprise (the dog expects the correction), or he does not know what to do or where to go. Determine what's wrong before continuing.

An effective correction is done **without emotion.** It comes with no warning. Then **Attention** or **Accuracy** is rewarded instantly.

No gushing praise or crazy play follows, just instant *reward* when Champ is correct. Allow him to think.

Maintain correct body posture. Suddenly grabbing the leash with two hands before correcting warns the dog.

Keep your usual tone of voice. Shouting the command only distracts from the correction. Keep cool, speak quietly and stay calm.

Handlers tend to get tense waiting for the moment to correct. Then the dog also gets nervous and starts anticipating the correction. This anxiety can create new problems, such as leaning and crowding in heeling.

Be especially sure your leash stays loose. Often handlers tense up and tighten the leash before a correction.

The dog feels this. He tenses up too in anticipation of a correction. And all this happens **before** there is ever any correction!

Stay loose before, and return to acting freely after the correction. Force must come from nothing and then result only in *reward* for correct behavior. Give your dog a chance to understand what the correction is for.

Calmness promotes learning. Stay **calm** to help your dog figure out how to avoid the correction through proper position and behavior.

Never correct anticipation! Anticipation is **always** the beginning of learning, never a disobedience. Your dog is trying to do what you want, what you have taught him.

Anticipation is normal (and can even be useful) during **Foundation** training. Later, the **Polishing** process eliminates any anticipation.

So just because your dog is doing something a little early, he doesn't deserve a correction! Add more *positive reinforcement* for the correct behavior (before he anticipates), and the problem disappears with training.

Patchwork

For the dog with a force foundation, maintain the behavior if it is correct. Add *motivation* to build *drive* and try to improve his **Attitude**, but be careful not to produce disobedience.

Remember to reinforce and *reward* only **Attention** and **Accuracy**. To get what he wants, the dog must do more than simply have a good **Attitude** and be having fun.

Corrections do not produce the same effect in this dog as in one with a motivational foundation. Force often produces tolerance to force.

The benefit of correction comes through **surprise**, not pain, and this dog already has his lasting *imprint* to compulsion. He can rarely be surprised. Different equipment can sometimes be effective for this dog, but only after some motivational training (without corrections).

Polishing

Force is being used correctly when the dog rebounds right back into *drive* and concentrates even harder for his *reward*. His black and white lines become clearer and the grey areas disappear.

Cooperative dogs high in *drive* can often complete their training through SchH. I, and even compete with "V" scores, without any corrections. The high V-scoring 1989 DVG National Champion in SchH. I was trained almost entirely in *play drive*, with only minor force to finish retrieving.

The entire process took two years though. So this does require patience.

When in doubt, always go back to motivational training for a secure **Foundation** before adding any sort of corrections.

7. YOUNG DOG
INVESTIGATES, . . . →

8. . . . AND GETS BORED.

9. DOG BECOMES
ATTENTIVE FOR FOOD, . . . →

10. . . . THEN GETS PUSHY
TO GET MORE FOOD.

Chapter 5

Getting Started

When training a dog, it is important
to leave it wanting to do more.
– Dr. Janet Ruckert

So now we are ready to get started. We need the right dog, the right equipment, the right place and a good idea of what we want to accomplish.

Goal: To create the correct *imprint* for the dog to the training field so he knows this is a place for **fun** and that he can drive the handler to get what he wants.

<u>When to Start</u>

Champ's age is not as important as his maturity level. He must be **ready** to work, both mentally and physically.

A growing dog is not coordinated. He barely knows he has a leg at each corner! He is clumsy.

Working a dog too early is like putting a 10-year-old child on a varsity athletic team. Neither is ready physically or mentally. They need to be finished with most of their growing before facing the demands of training.

Working a young dog does more damage than doing

nothing with him. The old adage, " No training is better than bad training, " certainly applies here.

Later training suffers when you start a dog too early. That all-important *imprint* to the training field can only be correct when Champ is mature enough and ready to handle the work.

In fact, the only real damage you can do to a good young dog is by doing too much too soon!

The dog must be in good *condition,* both physically and mentally, to function well in training. Quality food, clean water, fresh air, exercise and quiet time to rest are all necessary to maintain a successful working dog.

Sometime between 14 and 36 months, Champ shows that he is ready to work. Maturity varies greatly with breed, sex and genetic factors.

When a dog starts too young, he soon loses interest or gets distracted. This creates a poor first impression.

Young dogs can be **introduced** to certain elements of training, such as eating food from your hand or playing two hoses. But formal training must wait.

In going too far, too soon, the young dog gets stressed or quits and there is nothing you can do. This only teaches incorrect behavior and leaves him with the wrong idea. The dog must be mature enough to be an athlete.

The handler, also, must be an athlete. This is a **sport** and it requires that you be in good physical *condition* to participate. What you require of the dog is also required of the handler.

Equipment

Whatever Champ is going to wear in the course of training, it works best if he wears it from the start. So although it may be months before Champ gets his first correction, he starts wearing the appropriate collar **now**.

This makes his association with this collar positive. He is eager to "get dressed" for obedience. And he never associates any future correction with this collar because he has **always** worn it.

Please, no choke chains. Those small-link chain slip collars that go over the dog's head can be dangerous and inhumane, at worst. At best, they are ineffective.

A collar that chokes the dog can injure his throat. With a chain choker, it also takes too long to get an effectively timed correction.

It requires too much movement from the handler to be a **surprise** to the dog. The links even make a noise that warns the dog when a correction is coming.

But worse, if left on the dog and one ring catches on something, this collar can choke the dog to death.

To start, use a well-fitting fur saver collar. Attach the leash to the dead ring – the one that does not tighten the collar. Some extremely body sensitive dogs may even respond to eventual corrections on this collar.

A nylon snap-around collar, placed high on the neck (right behind the ears), gives an effective correction for some

---

(Terms appearing in *italics* are defined in the Glossary.)

medium sensitive dogs. This is also always used on the **dead** ring so it does not choke.

Please do not leave any choke collar on your dog. It can kill your dog quickly and is dangerous!

The most effective and humane collar for the great majority of working dogs is the prong collar, also known as the pinch collar. This fits snugly, high on the dog's neck, with both rings behind the dog's right ear. (See Fig. 6, Page 42.) When ready to use it, attach the leash to **both** rings of this collar, not just one.

There is no choking with this collar. Most handlers can be effective on this collar with very little arm movement.

The collar affects the entire area around the dog's neck, not just one spot. It also releases immediately.

But best of all, it cannot choke a dog to death!

The medium-sized prong collar is suitable for most dogs. (The smaller the size of the prongs, the more effective the correction.)

Those dogs with very heavy coats may need the large size collar since the prongs are longer. If the large collar is ineffective, however, the ends of the prongs can be made smaller.

Taper the last one-eighth inch of every other prong. Then flatten the ends so they cannot puncture the skin. This makes the larger collar more effective.

Remember, the value of a correction is in the element

of **surprise**, not in pain. Too much hand or leash movement and the shock value is lost.

A productive, motivational **Foundation** is the basis for successful obedience work, not corrections. We write this book in the hope that no dog ever needs to experience abusive compulsion again!

Use a leash only two to three-feet long attached to the dead ring of the fur saver collar. When you play with Champ and throw the hoses, be sure to remove the leash so the handle does not get caught in one of his legs.

The leash must be long enough to hold the handle (or slip it over your wrist), allowing Champ to heel in correct position with some slack in the line. (See Fig. 10, Page 54.) But it should not be so long that you have a wad of extra leash in your hand. And it must not hang down far enough to get tangled in your dog's legs.

You may want to invest in some equipment for yourself, too! A carpenter's apron or waist pouch is handy for holding hot dogs.

Overalls, or baggy pants with lots of pockets, offer places to store your hoses. If you don't want to get dirty from Champ jumping on you, coveralls (known as a "play suit" on our training field) allow you to fit in a few minutes of training, even in your good clothes.

If you have one of those hard-biting chow hounds, gloves come in handy (especially in colder weather when the bites hurt more!).

(Terms appearing in *italics* are defined in the Glossary.)   59

Commands

So now Champ is mature and he's outfitted with the right equipment. We must be ready to go to the training field. One more item.

Decide what commands you are going to use. German or English? A combination?

Here we will use the English commands for Heel, Sit, Down, Stand, Come, Fetch and Hup, but the German for Voraus.

The German commands are Fuss, Sitz, Platz, Steh, Hier, Brings, Hop and Voraus.

Whichever language you choose for training commands, select alternate ones for informal times. Commands on the training field are reinforced consistently. You expect Champ to follow them **immediately.**

If you use Down on the training field, you need an informal command. Relax or Lie can be used around the house (or anywhere else) as the informal command.

If Sit is your formal command, avoid using it off the training field. Especially avoid it for chores such as giving your dog medication or cutting his nails! You want him to expect something **pleasant** when he obeys the Sit command.

The same is true of Come. If you use the English in training, use the German Hier informally, or vice-versa.

The formal command means to come flying and sit straight in front. Your other command simply calls your dog over to you, or gets his attention when he's distracted or looking for trouble.

Each command means **specific** behavior. So avoid using Down when you want Champ to get Off the sofa, or to stop jumping up on your clean clothes.

Be consistent! Only then can Champ be sure he knows what each command means.

Where

Now we're off to the training field. Using the same place for all the sessions in Champ's **Foundation** training helps him learn more quickly.

Place association is the easiest way to teach Champ. He soon learns that in a certain place he does certain things.

Champ quickly recognizes and remembers familiar surroundings. This is natural and necessary in the wild. The wolf needs to know how to get back to the den after hunting many miles away. So he clearly remembers his surroundings even the first time he passes through.

Champ remembers places too. Take him back to a field where he once chased a rabbit. He'll go to that exact spot again, even if months have passed since he was there.

Use this natural ability to your advantage in training. Use the same field, the same starting point and the same **center line** until Champ understands the obedience exercises here.

A flat athletic field with short grass for smooth walking is the best place to start. Goalposts make good markers to help keep you on the center line. And eventually you can use one as a target for the voraus, too.

(Terms appearing in *italics* are defined in the Glossary.)   61

The center line itself is an important element in *place association*. Always use this center line for heeling, motion exercises, recall and voraus.

Start **every** exercise at the same spot each session, going in the same direction. This shows Champ what to expect, when and where.

Use this field for obedience **only**. For now, don't track here. Avoid letting Champ run free or relieve himself on this field.

Your dog is less distracted if you don't begin obedience training on the same field used for protection. However, if it is quiet and you are alone, he soon learns the difference.

The field you choose should be free from surrounding distractions. The quieter the better in the beginning.

We want to make a good *imprint* here. We want to create good habits. We want Champ to **enjoy** this place.

Beware of any negative *place association*. A young wolf in the wild learns the **first** time about skunks and thorns and snakes. Negatives make a strong *imprint*.

So your dog associates unpleasant experiences with places too. If something drastic goes wrong, consider changing location. Champ should look for food, play and enjoyment on the training field.

When

Short training sessions are better than long ones. Quit while Champ still wants more, long before he gets tired.

At first, even a mature dog doesn't have a long concentration span. This increases as training progresses.

As Champ builds *stamina* from playing two hoses, he can work longer. As his mental concentration gets better, he can learn more exercises.

To start, work Champ at least once each day, five times each week, or once every other day. If you have a job during the day and it is dark when you get home, find a lighted area. Or put up a light at home and work Champ for a few minutes each day, even if it has to be in your driveway.

This is much more effective at the start than working once or twice a week and making the sessions too long. Find time to work Champ **regularly** for brief periods in the beginning phases of training. This effort pays off because soon he can work longer and learn more exercises.

If you are lucky, and can work Champ twice a day, be sure to leave as much time as possible **between** sessions. There should be a minimum of four hours between each session. This must be quiet time for Champ, not running around with other dogs, the children or the family.

Isolate Champ for at least one-half hour before you take him training. This can be in the kennel or the crate. But he must be alone. This builds his desire to be with you.

After training, provide peace and quiet. Much learning goes on in the hour immediately following a training session, if you leave his mind free to absorb what has just happened.

Working Champ at the same time each day helps too. Going to the same place, at the same time each day, for the same training routine, gives Champ his best start in obedience.

(Terms appearing in *italics* are defined in the Glossary.)

Work Champ **before** you feed him. He is more eager for food. He is more lively at play. Besides, it is not healthy to work him energetically after he has eaten.

Foundation: Balances *food drive* and *play drive* so that both can be used during training. Helps the handler find out what motivates the dog best and develops the weaker *drive* so it can be functional within training. Makes the dog eager to go training because he always leaves wanting **more**.

First Session

Now we're ready to begin. Allow Champ to relieve himself away from the training field.

Put his prong collar high up on his neck. Attach the leash to the dead ring of the fur saver collar, which is below the prong on his neck.

The leash is **only** to keep Champ from running around. Walk around one end of the field, letting Champ investigate (Fig. 7, Page 54).

Stand still and wait until he gets bored with the environment (Fig. 8). Stand at your starting point and show him you have food (Fig. 9).

Feed him continuously for paying attention to you. If he starts pushing at your hand for the food, this is what you want (Fig. 10). Feed him **every** time he looks at you.

If you've done any tracking with your dog, he may start to look on the ground for the food. This is **not** a time for correction! Just keep showing him that the food is in your hand, not on the ground.

If he loses attention, do nothing. Just be ready and feed him the **moment** he looks back to you. Keep feeding as long as he is looking at you, and especially when he is driving you to give it to him.

As soon as he gets just a little more focused and pushy than he was at the start, feed him at his best moment and release him. Tell him Free, raise your arms up and move him away.

Then show him the hose. When he jumps for the hose or barks or otherwise starts to drive you for what he wants, take off his leash (if he won't run away) and play two hoses just for a few minutes. (You have already taught him this game.) Then snap his leash back on and walk off the field.

You have now made an important *imprint* on Champ in your first session. He knows this is a place for **fun.**

He knows you have what he wants. And he's learning that he can drive you to get it.

This first session is very short. You must end with Champ high in *drive* and wanting more. If he's nosing at your pockets and staring at you as you leave, you have done a good job.

If not, then repeat this session until Champ **does** start to drive you for what he wants. You want to see how strong his *food drive* and *play drive* are to find out what's going to work best.

If playing distracts your dog from focusing on food, then refrain from playing at all on the training field until later

---

(Terms appearing in *italics* are defined in the Glossary.)   65

exercises. This initial visit is to see how your dog responds and thus make adjustments in working your dog's drives.

You may have to repeat this first session several times before your dog's focus for food is continuous and he becomes pushy. Take as much time as he needs at this stage **before** beginning actual training.

You are starting to find out what happens when you push certain buttons. Champ's response to food and play during these first sessions, especially if it's in a new place, gives you a good reading on the strength of these two drives.

Ideally, you want to **balance** Champ's drives so you can use them both to your advantage during training.

If your dog plays hoses right away at this new field, but is more interested in them than in the food, then this is the last time you play hoses at the training field until it is specifically called for within an exercise. Develop his *food drive* more and allow him to concentrate on the food without any anticipation of play.

If your dog is so interested in the food that he doesn't switch readily to *play drive*, then you need more work away from the field to develop this weaker *drive*. Aim to strike the balance.

This first session is only to make the proper *imprint* on Champ and for you to evaluate his drives. Once you see how he responds, you know what to develop and whether you are ready to progress.

Remember, the leash is there **only** to stop your dog from escaping. There are miles to go with *motivation* before we start putting on the brakes.

Chapter 6

Happy Heeling

We are to listen to a dog until
we discover what is needed instead
of imposing ourselves in the name of training.
— Monks of New Skete

Goal: To produce energetic, enthusiastic movement in consistently correct position, the dog eagerly looking into the handler's face with absolute **Attention.**

Heel Position

Correct heel position is when the dog's shoulder stays in line with the left side of the handler's body. (See Fig. 11, Page 71.) All four feet (handler's and dog's) travel in the same direction.

The dog's body is straight, with his rear legs on the same track as his front feet. (See Fig. 12, Page 71.) His head can be turned just in front of your thigh to look at you, but his body remains straight.

If the dog's ribcage is ahead of your knee, he is forging. If his head is just even with the leading part of your body, he is lagging.

HEELING EXERCISE

From starting place on center line of field:
- Begin in basic position (sit). Acknowledge judge.
- 40 to 50 paces normal straight down center line, about turn.
- 10 paces normal, 10 fast, 10 slowly, 10 normal, right turn.
- 10 paces normal, right turn.
- 10 to 15 paces normal, about turn.
- 5 to 7 paces, halt.
- 5 to 10 paces, left turn and proceed to group.

All about turns are done to the left.

- Circle once to right around one moving person.
- Circle once to left around one moving person.
- Halt fairly close to one person.
- Leave group.

The circle done first may be in either direction.
The second circle must be done in the other direction.
The halt may be done between circles or after both circles.

SchH. I and II:
- 5 to 10 paces normal away from group, about turn.
- A few paces back toward group, halt. Remove leash.
- Repeat group as above off leash.
- Leave group off leash and proceed to center line starting point.
- Halt. Acknowledge judge. Repeat heeling exercise off leash.

SchH. III:
- Halt a few paces out of group or at center line starting point.

End of heeling exercise.

If he leans on your leg or interferes with your forward movement, he is crowding. If his shoulder is more than a few inches away from your leg, he is heeling too wide.

If his shoulder angles to the right in front of you and his rear swings out to the left, he is not heeling straight and tends to sit crooked. This wrapping in front of you also usually results in a forged heel position.

If his shoulder angles to the left (away from you), and his rear end swings in to the right (behind you), he is also heeling crooked and tends to sit crooked. This position usually leads to lagging.

Ideally, Champ looks up at your face. He watches your body movement, and where he is going, in his peripheral vision.

You look approximately 10 feet ahead. You plan where you are going and watch Champ in **your** peripheral vision (out of the bottom of your eyes).

Body Position

Your body is as upright as possible – shoulders square and relaxed. Looking down or back at your dog alters your body position. It provides an incorrect body cue and even **encourages** him to lag. Also, it can be marked as handler help in a trial.

Know where you are going. Be calm and concentrated, the way you want Champ to be. Push forward off the ball of your foot, making your legs do the work.

Try not to swing your upper body or hips from side to side. This creates excess body movement and slows you down.

All your energy and movement should be directed **forward** in a **straight** line. Swing your arms easily, only as much as feels comfortable to you.

69

With most dogs, the handler's left hand moving at your side comes too close to the dog's head, interfering with his **Attention** and distracting him. Be careful to hold you hands in a way that does not inhibit your dog from being in correct position and looking at you.

Practice walking properly **without** your dog. Pushing off smoothly and walking quickly uses new leg muscles, even for those athletic handlers who jog. Once you are comfortable walking this way, then you can begin with Champ.

Remember that you want to make the correct *imprint* for heeling. You can do this only if you are comfortable walking properly and know **exactly** where you want Champ to be.

Pattern Training

In Schutzhund, we are fortunate that the heeling pattern is basically the same every time. This allows us to teach Champ what to expect so he is **ready** for the next move.

By always using the same pattern, and feeding during or after each movement, Champ **wants** to make the next turn or change of pace, so he is ready. To teach this, keep each part of the pattern a little **shorter** than the actual exercise.

Soon, Champ begins to drive you to make the move he is expecting, so he can get the food. This makes him **more** attentive and intense.

In a trial routine, where the movements are a little longer than in training, Champ begins to drive you for the turn or change of pace he knows is coming. When he is at the peak of **Attention**, you oblige him by making the expected

11. CORRECT HEEL POSITION.

12. STRAIGHT HEELING.

move. He learns he can control what is happening and thus thoroughly enjoys the exercise.

There is no need to " trick and jerk " here. Champ **wants** to be correct. He learns what to expect and is ready to do it. There are no surprises for him in **Foundation** work.

You don't want to train the pattern? Neither did we. You want your dog to do **what** he is told **when** you tell him? So do we.

We had serious reservations about pattern training until we thought it through. Why shouldn't your dog know what to expect? You and your dog are a team, learning something new together. After your dog is fully trained, you can alter the pattern when you so choose.

In football, you tell your team members which play you are running. It's only the **other** team you want to fool!

The same applies to dog training. Let Champ **know** what you want, and then *reward* him for doing it. This fosters a reliable, enthusiastic team member. You'll be way ahead of the other team too!

Does pattern training cause anticipation? Certainly. But anticipation is merely the start of learning. Working it through is a simple matter of further training.

When a dog worries about what is going to happen, his mind gets blocked. He can't think. Teaching him what to expect eliminates his worry. He is free to learn.

Even when you train the " trick and jerk " method and mix up the pattern to fool the dog so you can correct him, it only lasts so long. By the time the dog has gone to two or three trials, and is ready to be competitive in SchH. III, he knows the routine. But there is no *motivation* for him to perform it properly, and no *reward* for learning it!

He begins to anticipate. He gets corrected for **trying** to do what you have taught him. He gets confused and depressed. Just what **do** you want of him?

Better for Champ to know the routine from the start and **enjoy** working this pattern because you give him something he likes at every turn (literally).

Some handlers say they train with *motivation* because they play ball with the dog at the end of an exercise. Even when we get a paycheck each Friday, we still work harder at those jobs that are **instantly** rewarding. Your dog enjoys his timely rewards too!

To train the pattern, you must **know** it first. (See Page 68.) This means walking it many times by yourself so you know exactly where you are going before asking Champ to come with you.

Foundation: Teaches the dog to get food by remaining attentive in correct position. Shows him what to expect when. Allows him to drive the handler for food. Makes the exercise enjoyable and rewarding for him.

First Session

Begin heeling when Champ meets the criteria outlined at the end of Chapter 5: Getting Started. He is hungry, eagerly takes food from your hand, and is ready to work.

Use a quiet field, with no distractions, where Champ is already comfortable. Put him on leash and walk around a

13. BEGIN WALKING WHILE
DOG IS LOOKING AT YOU.

14. KEEP FEEDING HAND
CLOSE TO YOUR BODY.

little bit near the starting position. (See Figs. 7 & 8, Page 54.)

When Champ looks to you, feed him from your hand. (See Fig. 9, Page 54.) Feed continuously while he looks to you. This rewards his **Attention.**

Try not to bait your dog. Show him the food once or twice so he knows you have it. Then feed him when he looks to you, or pushes your hand (Fig. 10, Page 54), or gives you his **Attention.**

While Champ looks at you or pushes you, lure him in closer to you as you feed him slices of hot dogs, one at a time (Fig. 13).

While Champ is close and looking at you, begin walking slowly, steering him into position at your left side. Feed him continuously when he is in the correct position. Keep your feeding hand and arm close to your body (Fig. 14).

The food is used as *positive reinforcement* (**while** he is heeling properly). This means you **feed** Champ the piece of hot dog (Fig. 16, Page 76), not just tease him with it.

Position your hand so that when Champ is at your left side and reaches his head up into the correct position, you feed him **without** moving your hand (Fig. 15).

Avoid reaching **down** or **back** to feed him. Your hand remains nearly still. Make Champ bring his head up into correct position to get the food.

Use the food to keep his head up above his shoulders. If he tries to sit down, walk just a little faster to prevent this.

These first few steps are critical. Keep feeding correctly

so that Champ's head stays up (Fig. 15). He needs to learn how to walk with his head up. This is not a natural position for a dog.

Walk slowly only the first few steps. As soon as he begins to master the technique, speed up and walk quickly. Feed him **continuously** as he maintains proper heel position (Fig. 15).

15. FEED WHEN DOG IS
IN CORRECT HEEL POSITION.

16. FEED CONTINUALLY
TO KEEP YOUR DOG'S HEAD UP.

17. CONTINUAL FEEDING
STABILIZES HEEL POSITION.

These first few sessions are critical, but also difficult. You have much to do – reading Champ, watching his behavior, steering him into correct position, keeping your body upright, walking a straight line, feeding at just the right instant – and all at the same time!

For most dogs, feed from your left hand. Keep the food in a pouch or pocket just **above** the level of Champ's head, on your **left** side.

Keep your **Goal** and your perfect picture in mind. Guide Champ into that perfect position by steering him with food (Fig. 15). Feed him continuously when he is correct.

You can sacrifice perfect body posture these first few sessions in favor of Champ being in correct position. But be aware of the compromise in using body language and wean yourself away from it quickly.

Words are not really important at this point. You can say Heel, Good Dog if you are comfortable doing that (and don't already have enough to remember).

If you do need to say something, be sure to say Heel only when Champ is **in** correct position, not to bring him **into** position. We are *shaping* behavior here and creating word association, not ordering him into place.

If talking distracts your dog initially, stop. He's concentrating on getting that food he wants. Introduce the words later, when he's more sure of the technique.

If your leash gets in your way, tuck the end in the left side of your belt or loop it over your arm. Be sure it is slack.

There should be no leash tension to create *opposition reflex*. But it should not hang down far enough to get tangled in your dog's feet. Remember, the leash is there only to keep him near you, not to guide or correct.

Champ wears his prong collar. But the leash attaches to the dead ring of his fur saver for all **Foundation** training.

If Champ has had some tracking experience and wants to search for food on the ground, walk a little faster and show him the food in your hand. Feed him more from your hand until he learns **that's** where it's coming from now.

In this case, if the leash gets tight, just say his name and show him the food in your hand (*motivation*). Feed him whenever he gets close beside you and keep going.

If your dog jumps up to grab the food, or leaps for sheer joy, say nothing. Keep walking briskly. Just ignore it.

He gets no food because he is out of position. Be sure not to reprimand him or correct him just for having too much **fun**!

Be sure your hand is in the right place (Fig. 15). When he lands on the ground again, feed him the **instant** he is in the correct position and keep feeding as long as he stays there (Fig. 15).

For most dogs, it works best to carry your food stash just **above** the dog's eye level – on your left side. This encourages Champ to look **up** as you reach for more food, but not wrap around you. Reaching down low into a pants pocket, or over to your right side, can focus him on where the food comes from and begin a bad habit.

Storing the food too high encourages your dog to jump up to get at the food. Carrying the food at waist level usually works best. For a dog who tends to lag, you may want to try feeding from your right hand and keeping the food on your right side for a few sessions, to create better position.

These are just a few examples of finding **what works** for your dog!

All correct heeling in position results in *positive reinforcement* (food **while** he is performing properly, not **after**). Ignore any other action.

Especially reinforce Champ's behavior every time he looks into your eyes while in correct position. This is part of our ultimate **Goal** and we want to encourage it now.

Discipline has no place here. And avoid clucking or whistling or attracting him with anything but the food.

He needs to be allowed to think. Through concentrating, he learns how to get what he wants.

This never happens if you help him all the time. Unnecessary noises and actions distract the dog. They either interfere with his concentration or he comes to rely upon them.

Be patient. Be positive. Be persistent. Concentrate fully on Champ so you offer food at **exactly** the right moment and avoid mistakes.

Creating the correct heeling habit takes time. Resolve to persevere with your dog and get it right, not just to try.

Remember, you are *shaping* Champ's behavior. (See Chapter 2: How?) Every correct effort or response results in *positive reinforcement*. Champ gets what he wants **as soon as** he does something right.

Form good habits in the beginning. Walk quickly and positively down the center line. Be calm and concentrated.

Watch Champ's reactions and observe his behavior. Soon you begin to see what he is going to do **before** he does it and your timing gets perfect.

Use the long straight center line to keep Champ's **Attention** with the food. Get into a rhythm with him. Get comfortable walking at the correct pace (quickly), feeding and working with Champ as a team.

When you get to the end of the center line, make one-half a small circle to the **right** the first few sessions. Keep Champ in position by bringing the food just a little more toward the center of your body. Return down the center line.

Continue reading and feeding Champ, building a rhythm and rapport together. Your center line here is about 30 paces long – just slightly **shorter** than trial routine.

If Champ was **super** and fell into **perfect** heel position and the entire exercise went smoothly the first time, we hope you made a video. You **both** deserve a prize!

Even if that was the case, once down and back is enough for this first attempt. Release Champ from heeling at his **best** moment. Use food or a toy in your hand as you throw your hands up and use your release word. Start now to develop an explosive, energetic release. Jump forward two or three steps as you raise your hands, encouraging Champ to jump and focus **up**.

If heeling didn't quite go as well as expected, release him anyway and regroup. You both need a breather from your first effort. Walk off the center line and relax for a minute or two.

After any release, allow Champ to jump on you and be a free dog. This is **his** time, so avoid nagging.

Avoid wild praise or exuberant petting after the release. Both need to be earned. Save your praise and petting so they are meaningful to Champ **within** the exercise. You'll be needing them soon enough.

If you think Champ is really ready for more, and you're excited rather than frustrated, repeat the same procedure. One more time down and back, then release at his best moment. Now you're done for this session.

You can play two hoses with Champ along the center line, with you in the middle. Play just long enough to increase his *stamina* a little, but stop while he still wants **more**. (Play only if it does not diminish his response to food for the next session.)

End your first session, no matter how much **you** want to continue. Stop even if you just figured out what you **should** have done! Learn right now to resist the One-More-Time Syndrome.

Champ now goes back to a **quiet** place by himself. That can be his crate, or his kennel, or anywhere there is no noise and no visual stimulation. This especially means no children and no other dogs.

Give him at least one hour to settle down and relax. Surprising as it may seem, significant learning and absorption of what has just happened goes on in this quiet time **immediately after** training. Your training progresses much faster when you provide it.

If nothing else, Champ learns that training is the **fun** time. Letting him play with other dogs after training, or just going for a walk in the woods, only teaches that better things might happen **after** training.

Channel all his *drive* and enthusiasm into the training session itself.

<u>Wiener Warning</u>

Caution: hot dogs are fattening! If you're feeding Champ a wad of wienies at each training session (which you should), be sure to compensate by decreasing his food. Cut each meal in **half** for the first few weeks. We don't want him too fat to get over the jump when we get to that exercise!

Besides fat, hot dogs contain numerous food by-products, fillers, additives and preservatives. Some dogs are allergic to these ingredients. Low-fat turkey franks often suit their systems better.

Why use hot dogs? They slice nicely into nickel-shaped pieces. Used whole, they fit perfectly into most hands to allow Champ to nibble on the end. They are readily available. They are soft and require no chewing.

String cheese is also convenient. But if you choose another food, be sure it's not crunchy or hard. We don't want the dog taking time to chew and losing concentration. Harder food or smaller treats can get stuck in a dog's throat if he inhales them.

Some students have even invented "wienie machines" for feeding the dog without getting their fingers bitten. We're still waiting for the prototype of a wiener slicer to produce perfect nickel-width pieces with one stroke!

The Heeling Habit

Continue this heeling program until Champ is consistently getting in the right position and giving you his full **Attention** to get fed. If you are feeding correctly, each session gets smoother and more rhythmical.

For a dog who tries to forge ahead of you, heel in a **big** circle to the **left** for a few sessions. Keep the food only in your **left** hand and close to your waist so it steers the dog **back** into position.

Use your upper body turned to the left slightly to keep him back. No hard bumping with your knee. Let him discover how to get what he wants.

For a dog who naturally lags a little, heel in a **big** circle to the **right**. Try the food in your **right** hand, near the center of your body, so his head **must** come up to get it. Keep your upper body turned slightly to the right to get him to work harder to get at the food.

This dog may be a little unsure, not the pushy kind. Encourage him a little more. Show him the food a few times and guide him into the right position. Praise and reassure him as well as feeding him there. Work more on building his *drive* off the training field.

For a dog who wants to swing his rear end out to the left, keep the food in your **left** hand. Steer his head into position slightly out to the **left** so his front and rear track straight beside you.

Keep your elbow in to keep him close. Use the **left** circle a few times for this dog too, to teach him to keep his rear end in.

Steering with food sounds **simple**. It is a simple idea. But, it is not **easy**. It is always amazing just how creative a dog can be trying to get the food!

Realize that this is a new technique for you too. Persist until you get it right and you will be well rewarded.

Happy heeling becomes a habit. Stabilizing the behavior takes months, not weeks. But this time is so well spent.

Heel position is the basis for all other exercises. When Champ is happy and secure in heel position, you start on a solid **Foundation** that lasts through all your training together.

As Champ begins to maintain position and focus on you constantly, say Heel **while** he is in correct position. When you feed him, calmly tell him Heel, Good Dog.

If even this much talking still distracts him, wait until he has more experience. When he understands more clearly what is expected, and has learned exactly how to maintain position to get the food, he quickly learns what Heel means.

Then add quiet praise when you feed him. Associating praise with food makes them both more meaningful to Champ. Later, when the food doesn't come, praise has a very **positive** association. He knows he's right and that soon his *reward* will come.

While adding Heel and praise, work on rhythmical feeding while heeling up and down the center line. Continue to release Champ after each pattern of down and back and take a quick breather.

You can repeat down and back **twice** in each session, provided Champ stays in *drive*. This simulates the double pattern of on-leash and off-leash heeling in SchH. I and II.

Rhythmical feeding means that, with every third or fourth step, you feed Champ when he is correct.

Keep your speed consistent. No surprises. Make Champ clear, correct and confident along this center line.

Walk as fast as is necessary to keep your dog in a smooth trot. Free forward movement from you makes Champ more free. Speed increases **Attention.**

Speed means striding out farther and longer, not hectic body movement. Your energy must be clearly channeled **forward** so Champ channels that direction too.

About Turn

When Champ is heeling up and down the center line with **Attention** and **Accuracy,** teach a correct about turn. **All** about turns at this point in training are done to the **right.** This is the same about turn used in AKC obedience trials.

Teach Champ the correct technique first. Once he learns to take the **shortest** route around you, his about turns are fast and smooth and he stays in correct position.

Left about turns, those used in trial, come later. Champ must **learn** to stay close to your body as he comes around. Going wide takes longer and never looks as smooth.

Champ does **his** turn the same way, even when **you** do

a left about turn. But it is difficult to guide your dog smoothly around your body when you go left and he goes right.

Once he learns the technique of how to go around, he is fast and smooth in the turn no matter which way **you** go. He learns the technique by doing the turn slowly, always to the **right**, in **Foundation** training.

Practice the turn without Champ first. Keep your feet underneath you and your body upright.

Take two or three small steps to turn around. If you pivot on one foot and then step out with the other in the opposite direction, you're sure to leave your poor dog in the dust.

You can speed up your turn and improve your handling after Champ learns the proper technique. For now, teach it **slowly** and give him a chance. Keep him beside you, in correct position, all the way around the turn.

Remember, we're not trying to trick him. We want to **show** him how to turn properly the **first** time.

As you approach the end of your 30 paces down the center line, show Champ a piece of food and be sure he is attentive. Move the food **slowly** slightly to the right, more to the center of your body than usual.

Keep the food close to your body, right in front of where you want his nose to be. Guide Champ around the turn this way so he learns correct technique.

Use the food just above his nose, so he keeps his head up. As you finish the turn, feed him after your **first** step in the other direction. Add praise with the food as soon as he starts to get it right.

Champ learns that the closer and faster he gets around the turn, the quicker he gets the food. *Reward* **every** about turn after your first stride in the opposite direction.

He finds out that the shortest route around you is also the fastest way to the food. He learns correct technique and begins a good habit.

If your dog gets out of position, chalk it up to handler error. He **can't** possibly be wrong because he doesn't know what's right yet!

If he does get out of position, keep showing him the food close to your body and feed him **immediately** when he hits correct position down the center line. Next time, add more food *motivation* **just before** your turn. Turn only when your dog is in full **Attention.**

Slow down a little more and guide him carefully around the turn so he finds the shortest (and thus fastest) route around you. *Reward* after the first step in the opposite direction, keeping your hand close to your body.

From now on, *reward* **every** about turn after your first step in the opposite direction, or as soon as Champ is in correct heel position going in the new direction.

Right and Left

Once Champ is close and smooth on about turns, add the right and left turns into the pattern. The technique is similar.

Use food *motivation* **just before** you are going to turn. Turn only when Champ is in full **Attention.**

Show him the food. One stride before, turn your upper body and look in the direction you are going to go.

Exaggerate this body cue at first. Champ soon picks up on this indication even when it is much more subtle.

Keep your feet underneath you. Stay balanced and upright, not leaning. Look in the direction you want to go so you make a **square** turn.

Feed after your **first** step in the new direction. Then proceed in a straight line in that direction according to the pattern so Champ can get his new bearings on the field.

Take two small steps to get around a right turn at first. You'll lose your dog if you pivot too fast. Keep both turns slightly slower until Champ learns the correct technique.

Praise during and feed after **every** turn when Champ is in correct position. When Champ expects his *reward* after each turn, and then he learns the pattern, he starts driving you to turn so he can get fed.

Remember, this is not " trick and jerk." In motivational training, you turn **only** when Champ is paying attention and is **ready** for the turn.

Teach turns this way and you'll be surprised at the **Attention** and **Accuracy** you produce, while developing an eager **Attitude**.

Change of Pace

Once Champ has a good grasp of correct heel position, incorporate the fast pace into the routine. After your right about turn, take at least 10 normal paces before starting your fast. This defines your center line again and prevents Champ from forging after the about turn.

Before speeding up, lean forward slightly with your upper body. Use this cue consistently and Champ is **always** ready for the change of pace.

Stretch the dog out slowly instead of leaping into the fast gait. Increase your speed gradually until Champ breaks from a trot to a canter.

For your first several fasts, continue running to the end of the field and then release Champ from heeling. Use a really dynamic release – throwing your arms up as you give your release command. This long fast pace becomes extremely motivational for the dog.

The speed makes him feel free and excited. You want Champ to enjoy the fast pace and perform at a lively speed.

Slowing down after 10 paces teaches him to prepare to slow down before he's even up to fast speed. You want him to keep running with you and **enjoy** the feeling.

You also need to practice proper position. Getting coordinated with Champ at a fast run can be challenging. (See Fig. 22, Page 117.) Continuing the fast all the way to the end of the field gives you more time to get the rhythm right.

Continue feeding during the entire fast pace to keep Champ in proper position. At first it may be difficult to keep his focus when he's having so much fun, but practice working together as a team even at your top speed.

If he leaps up or jumps out of position, stop feeding

and slow down. To get the **fun** of running, Champ must stay in position.

If he starts getting really crazy, laugh and smile and shake your head. Slow down, get his **Attention** and start over.

Isn't it wonderful!? You and Champ are having **fun.** Yes, he's having a little **too** much fun right now. But let's not tell him that just yet.

You'll have plenty of time to take the wind out of his sails! Putting that wind back in is much more difficult.

So avoid correcting him in any way, even with a sharp voice. Remember that he's still just **learning** proper heel position.

As soon as Champ masters the proper heeling position at the fast pace, begin to shorten your running to about 15 or 20 paces. Now teach the transition.

Just before slowing down, lean back somewhat with your upper body and relax your shoulders. Exaggerate this cue at first. Begin by taking five or six strides to change back to normal pace.

Make your Heel command here quiet and slow, in a low tone of voice. This also helps Champ know what's happening.

Ease into the slow pace. If you downshift too fast, you'll surprise your dog and the movement looks choppy. Or he might try to sit. **Prevent** mistakes by being prepared.

Feed Champ in correct position throughout the transition. As he gets better, shorten the transition to only two or three paces.

Always feed for the first few normal steps after the transition. This prepares Champ to pay attention during the slow pace.

The full-length slow pace can be ignored for now. It's not very motivational and comes naturally once heel position is correct and Champ knows the technique of the transition.

After heeling at the fast pace is stabilized, you can add a **few** paces of slow to the routine once in a great while. (This is mostly to make the handler feel better.)

Feed Champ constantly to keep him interested in this boring slow stuff. Before you see him losing interest, speed up to normal pace. Get his **Attention** again and put him back in *drive* before making your right turn.

The Group

Once your heeling pattern is fairly stable, prepare Champ for the group. Incorporate this into the routine after the right and left turns so Champ knows when to expect it.

The first time through a group of people, walk a straight line. Increase your speed and feed him more to keep Champ's attention on you.

The people should be quiet and still. Be sure Champ finds **you** the most interesting person in the group. At first, stay several feet away from any of the individuals.

Once Champ is keeping his focus on you through the group, the people can begin moving slowly your next time through. When attention and position are perfect, pass within a few feet of the individuals, still keeping Champ's attention by feeding.

Absolutely no corrections are made for **Attention** within the group. You want Champ to look confident and secure in the group, not worried about what might happen.

When Champ's heeling performance in the group is consistently correct, add the halt with continuous feeding in this position. (See Chapter 7: The Solid Sit.) Once you master these basics, continue training for the specific pattern within the group.

<u>SV Group</u>

Even though most of your **Foundation** training is done without other people, you can still teach the technique and pattern of the group. Use traffic cones, chairs, sticks or trees to mark the position of your group when you are by yourself.

For the SV group, you must show one full circle to the right around one of the four (or five) milling people, one halt, and one full circle to the left around another person. Execute the **same** routine **every** time, again so Champ knows where you're going and is ready.

Enter the group on a **straight** line. Begin arcing **gently** to the right so Champ figures out you've started turning in that direction.

Increase feeding while you make this circle to the right. Tighten up the circle as you come around the object or person.

Just as you finish your circle to the right – feed, praise and then release Champ with much energy and enthusiasm. Releasing here builds intensity for the right turn in the group.

Once Champ is heeling with good **Attention** and **Attitude**, and is accurate in the group, add the halt.

Take a few straight steps out of your right-hand arc and halt in the middle of the group, on a **straight** line. Feed continuously during this sit. (See Chapter 7: The Solid Sit.)

The first few times you add the sit, hold it for several seconds. Feed, praise and then release with great energy and enthusaism.

When the right circle and sit are correct, add the left circle. From a solid sit, held for several seconds, start immediately to the left, turning your upper body slightly and looking in the direction you are going.

When you do this each time, Champ knows you **start** to the left after this halt. Then he doesn't bump on that first step to the left.

Arc to the left **slowly**, feeding constantly from your left hand (just slightly further back than usual) to keep Champ in correct position. Gradually tighten the turn as you complete your circle around the second object or person. Continue adding the left circle each training session until Champ gets the idea.

Leave the group in a straight line and release. Play two hoses for a few seconds here.

Left circles are like slow pace, they lack energy and tend to be boring. Keep them to a minimum, especially if your dog tends to lag, or if he's lazy rather than crazy.

You might have the opposite problem. If your dog is overly enthusiastic about everything and you're falling over him to the left, exaggerate the food further back. Go slowly until he figures out how to get out of your way and get the food.

With a forging or bumping dog, use this left circle more and make it tighter so he **learns** to get out of your way. This dog also probably needs more work on slow pace than most.

Add a halt outside the group with enthusiastic dogs. Releasing from heeling can excite them too much. They need the calming effect of a halt for several seconds before being released.

When practicing the group with people, avoid going too close at first. Decrease the distance when his focus on you is absolute. Remember to make **yourself** the most interesting person in the group.

DVG Group

In the DVG group, you heel straight between two lines of people moving back and forth across your path. Proceed about five paces out of the group in a straight line and make an about turn. You then return and halt within the group.

Practice first with the people standing still. Make **yourself** the most interesting person there by walking faster and feeding more continuously. After the group, release with energy and enthusiasm.

Once Champ keeps his focus on you, have the people begin moving, slowly at first. As Champ becomes more attentive, have the group move closer and then cross back and forth.

Add the halt (with continuous feeding) within the group as you progress. (See Chapter 7: The Solid Sit.) Keep Champ's **Attention** with more food than usual.

Walk out of the group before releasing Champ. Then play a little as you return to your starting point to run through the second heeling pattern (no group).

Play after the group **only** if it does not distract your dog from focusing on the food in proper position. Only a dog with balanced drives can switch between food and play readily.

The group provides the highest distraction for your dog, so be sure to convince him that **you** are more interesting than them. You do that by adding more *motivation*.

Lagging in the group is a common sight. Many dogs get tired or bored with heeling by this point. Corrections in the group can make a dog look nervous and insecure.

But when Champ is energized here after each release, his **Attention** increases where it normally would diminish. His **Attitude** blossoms and he shifts into overdrive!

It is normal for a social dog, or for one of the guarding breeds, to want to check out the people in the group, either by looking or sniffing. Correcting the dog for this natural behavior is unfair. He comes to anticipate correction in the group and so he gets worried. This is the **exact opposite** of the picture you want to present!

Use *motivation* here consistently to make yourself much more interesting than anyone else in the group. Move quickly and surely in the group so you present the picture of a confident team.

Fumbling Practice

When you and Champ are comfortable with your group pattern, begin preparing to take off your leash. Leave the group in a straight line.

Make an about turn after at least 15 or 20 paces. Halt about half way back to the group.

Steer Champ into a solid, straight sit and feed. (See Chapter 7: The Solid Sit.) **Practice** reaching for the leash snap.

With your right hand, reach down and just touch the snap at first. Feed Champ from your left hand so he maintains correct position during this process.

In successive sessions, progress to fumbling with the snap, clicking it open and closed without removing the leash, until Champ maintains position and **Attention.** Then snap it off and right back on, while your hand is still at the collar.

This practice is as much for you as it is for Champ. Removing the leash is one of the most bungled parts of the SchH. I and II routines.

Unsnapping the leash and keeping Champ in position while you put it away require practice and preparation. It gets even harder when you're nervous in a real trial!

Feed Champ whenever he is still paying **Attention** and in correct position. Champ learns that your fumbling with the snap doesn't necessarily mean he's going to be a free dog.

If your dog does try to shoot off at any point, simply let him hit the end of the leash. Bring him back into proper position with food. Feed him when he finally arrives back there. He soon finds out where his advantage lies.

After you practice fumbling, be sure Champ is in **Attention**. Return to the group and repeat the pattern.

Notice that we are **not** actually removing the leash in heeling at this point. We are still building a solid **Foundation**.

We're still training! Off-leash heeling is testing. We'll begin testing only when:

- **Foundation** is nearly complete.
- **Goal** is almost accomplished.
- **Attention** is absolute.
- **Accuracy** is perfect.
- **Attitude** is enthusiastic.

All the **Foundation** is done with *motivation*. Keep working on this until the entire pattern is picture perfect. Once we're happy with the picture, we begin proofing.

Proofing

By now Champ is a happy heeler and doing almost a full routine. His *condition* is getting better and his *stamina* has increased.

He's beginning to understand heel position. He knows **exactly** what's coming next and he drives you to do it so he can get his *reward.*

You feel comfortable knowing what he's going to do. Motivating, reinforcing and rewarding are becoming habits.

Until now, all the heeling has been done on a quiet field, preferably your original training field. If you must go to different locations before your **Foundation** is finished, back up a few steps in each new place and add more *motivation*.

Proofing really means **proving** that Champ knows what to do and can concentrate despite new situations or distractions. While proofing, we press him a little harder, but still with *motivation*, not with correction.

First add a few new distractions, **one** at a time, on your original training field during heeling. These can include another dog on the long down, someone playing judge and walking around the field, another team working at the side of the field, a windy day when objects are blowing across the field, children playing on the sidelines, gunfire from a distance (pre-test dog elsewhere for sound sensitivity and gunshureness), a small group of people talking and laughing together on the field, someone shouting, a jump falling over, people calling and chasing a seemingly loose dog along the end of the field, large marker flags flapping in the wind where the long down would be, one blind on the side of the field (with or without a person sitting in it), trucks or motorcycles driving along a nearby road, a golf cart or mini-bike driving across the field, a loud boom-box turned on suddenly, feedback from a public address system, or someone with a squawking parrot on his shoulder walking around.

Well, you get the idea. Obviously you don't need to proof for all these things, but use your imagination.

Those listed here didn't have to be imagined. They've **all** actually happened at one time or another at a trial we've attended!

Anything that **could** happen at a trial is legal. This does **not** include ball throwing, Frisbee games, another dog chasing hoses or a loose dog on the field.

You're trying to proof Champ, not trick him into making a mistake. You're **showing** him what could happen and adding *motivation* to be sure he still concentrates on you.

Add only **one** distraction per session. Avoid overload. Keep your routine short and stimulating.

The more strange situations he successfully survives on his home field, the more confident and concentrated he becomes. Once he sees a couple of new distractions, and you conquer his lapses with *motivation*, Champ begins to ignore whatever else is happening on the field. If his *temperament* is stable, he quickly forgets the environment and devotes himself to his work.

No corrections are allowed here because that would produce exactly the **opposite** result to what we want. If a dog gets corrected every time he tries to look at something new, he soon gets worried and unsure. He anticipates the correction whenever he notices a change in the situation.

This is the same reason we don't correct the dog for inattention in the group. We want Champ sure of himself, cocky and confident in any new situation.

We want to be the **good guy** in new situations. We want Champ to think of us as the **safest** and most **fun** person around.

100

We are the team member, not the villain. We are his security. We want to be his salvation, not his persecution.

Whenever we introduce a distraction on purpose, we add *motivation*. Have the distraction present **before** you begin heeling.

Let Champ see (or hear) what is there, from a distance, before you ask him for **Attention**. Dogs are naturally curious about their surroundings. It goes against their nature not to notice something new or different.

Once you get his **Attention** and begin heeling, break up the exercise with release and play more often than you normally would. This gives Champ another chance to check out the situation.

He can then be more intense when you get back to work. He also begins to believe that new situations mean more fun!

When he's secure on his home field, he's ready for field trips. On a new field, go back to basics.

Walk around with him and let him sniff and investigate. Wait until he drives you to do something before you start heeling.

Use a field without new distractions – a quiet place that is just different. If you work at a school athletic field or sports complex, another field at the same site is ideal.

Keep the pattern even **shorter** than usual. Use more *motivation* and more breaks for play than normal.

If anything goes wrong with heeling, or any other exercise, back up to Show and Tell. Show Champ what to do, then Tell him he's a Good Dog and feed him.

If distractions at home and new fields don't faze Champ, add new and unusual situations. Horses, cows or sheep grazing in view of the training field really interest some dogs. A field at a kennel, where many dogs are barking, can distract others. Planes or trains going by might break concentration.

Each new experience, when overcome through *motivation*, gives you both confidence. You rely on each other and teamwork improves.

Proofing makes you both more sure you can survive the unexpected in a trial. It puts you one big step closer to success!

Off-Leash Heeling

After proofing, you have a good idea of Champ's level of understanding of heel position. You've seen his attention span.

If you're happy with Champ's performance, you can begin to **test** the full heeling routine. This means taking off the leash.

Begin back on your home field with **no** distractions. Do the first heeling pattern on leash, keeping *motivation* high, but with slightly less feeding than usual. Make the pattern just a little shorter than normal – 20 paces instead of 30.

After leaving the group and halting, remove the leash. By now Champ is already used to your fumbling here.

Your **Foundation** training relied so little on the leash that it usually doesn't make much difference to Champ whether it's on or off. (He doesn't even know what it's **for** yet!) But the leash can be a big security factor for the handler.

If you have any worries about taking it off, have a thin piece of line already attached to his fur saver and to your belt as a safety measure (known as an umbilical cord). But if you're not sure what your dog will do, you really aren't ready to try heeling off-leash.

Return to your starting position, keeping Champ's interest. While heeling off-leash, feed **much more** during the pattern.

Make your first off-leash pattern successful. Keep it short, especially if you get nervous that something might go wrong.

Mix up whether you heel the second pattern off-leash during training sessions. A good ratio is one in five for testing an off-leash pattern, but **only** if all is going well on-leash.

<u>Weaning from Food</u>

By now you and Champ are working well together. Most of the other exercises already have a solid **Foundation**.

You start looking ahead to a trial where you can enter Champ. You're getting excited with anticipation, and a little nervous too, naturally.

All of a sudden the big question pops up: " What is Champ gonna do when there's no food?!"

You're right! It **is** risky business to go to trial without testing Champ on heeling without food.

We've seen it enough now to know that it **can** work, but we were skeptical for a long time too. We certainly don't advise it. And we don't expect you to be an instant believer either.

Begin on your home field. Replace food reinforcement with *motivation*. **Show** Champ the food for half a leg, but don't give it to him until he really gets intense and tries harder, still staying in position.

This teaches Champ to work harder for what he wants. It convinces him he **will** get it eventually if he's correct and attentive.

Motivation such as this often increases *drive* in an intense dog with a strong **Foundation.** Many working dogs react by looking into your eyes – at first questioning, then driving you to give them the food. When you first see Champ try to drive you by looking intensely into your eyes, praise and positively reinforce the behavior **immediately.**

Give Champ the food about half way down the first leg, when he is in his best position. Then return to rhythmical feeding. Continue to *reward* **every** turn.

The next two or three patterns, return to your regular feeding during heeling. You can add some slight distractions these sessions, or train at a new field, but maintain rhythmical, regular feeding during heeling.

Back on your home field again, with no distractions, feed Champ in sit position at the starting point. Heel to the end of the center line **without** using food. Praise Champ calmly when he is attentive and correct.

Just before turning, show Champ the food. Guide him around the turn and *reward* as usual. Continue the heeling pattern, feeding as you usually do.

This teaches Champ that, even when the food isn't there at the start, it comes fairly soon. Once in every five training sessions, train part of the heeling pattern without food.

On days when Champ is at his best, heel for half one leg without food. Sessions when you or your dog aren't quite in gear, keep food as usual.

Always feed Champ **instantly** when you see him make intense eye contact to drive you into giving him what he expects, provided he remains in correct position. This is the behavior we want.

Occasionally, when all other training is going well, practice one heeling pattern feeding Champ **only** on turns, transitions and halts. This shows you his attention span and gives you a clear picture of how he will look on trial day.

Beware of weaning off food too much, especially right before trial day. Give yourself plenty of time to return to training sessions which reinforce regularly with food.

Once you build a motivational **Foundation**, the *motivation* is almost always there. Teaching Champ consistently what to **expect**, creating the habit and then rewarding correct behavior, are the most important elements in this training program.

In any training program, the reinforcement must **always** be there, whether positive or negative. Otherwise, you are testing, not training.

Keep giving Champ what **he** wants in training, and he rewards **you** with consistent top performance.

Left About Turns

With your eye on trial day now, it's time to teach Champ the left about turn. By now the other exercises are secure.

You have already guided Champ behind you with food while teaching the finish (See Chapter 12: Front to Finish). As you come to the end of heeling down your center line, Champ **knows** you're going to do an about turn.

Slow down slightly. Techniques are taught slowly, not quickly. Speed comes with understanding and experience.

Show Champ food in your **left** hand. Transfer it to your **right** hand just in front of Champ's nose. As you do this, you naturally turn your upper body to the left. You go left as he goes right.

Guide Champ around with the food. Keep your feet underneath you and your body upright, just as you did when first teaching the right about turn.

Transfer the food to your **left** hand behind your back, holding it just **above** Champ's nose to keep his head high as he comes around. Feed him the **moment** he arrives in heel position on the other side of you.

Continue heeling back down the center line and practice it again at the other end. Forget the pattern and other turns for now, just work up and down two or three times (about 20 paces) until you start to get a smooth, sure turn.

After a good about turn to the left, continue heeling for four or five paces down the center line and then release. End the session there for today. Be sure to give Champ his quiet time after training, especially when you've introduced something new.

Be patient with this move. Practice it slowly until Champ is sure of his technique. Turning your body to the left may confuse him at first. Just continue guiding him with the food until he gets it.

Once the left about turn is smooth, use it approximately every third turn in different places (at the end of field or between right and left turns), provided his turns remain close, fast and correct. Continue to use the right about turn more often to be sure he keeps coming around correctly.

Play Drive

Using *play drive* for about turns can make the dog quick around the turn, but it rarely produces smoothness and correct technique. Usually, the dog swings wide on the turn (out of position) and then dives back beside you.

He rarely hits correct heel position on the first stride, however. He is usually wide, or he forges, because he's going too fast or anticipating play.

You want Champ to stay close to you at all times. The fastest way around is for him to turn tightly and stay close to your body. Then he arrives in **correct** heel position because he always remained close to you.

Besides, you can reinforce correct heel position immediately with food as the dog comes around the turn. With play, you can only *reward* the dog for an action he has completed, and while playing he is out of position. Then you

18. HOSE PLACEMENT
PRODUCES CORRECT HEELING.

19. REWARDING WITH HOSE
IN THE CORRECT POSITION.

have to get your dog to give up the hose, calm down and get back into position to continue with heeling.

Using *play drive* during heeling is tricky, but it can work with some dogs. The trick is to get the hose in the proper place.

Motivate Champ with the hose. Experiment while walking to see which hose placement puts him in correct heel position. (See Fig. 11, Page 71.) Most often, carrying the hose in your **left** hand and putting it just above his head on your **left** side, produces correct heel position with Champ looking up (Fig. 18).

Whenever using the hose, *reward* in correct heel position by letting him bite it (Fig. 19) **before** he starts to forge. Insist on correct position and tell him to Get It just as you lower the hose and allow him to bite it. Watch your fingers!

That way he knows he can't jump for it whenever he wants. Put it in his mouth while he is as close to heel position as possible (Fig. 19).

After a short tug-of-war, tell him Heel and make him **let go** of the hose. You stop tugging too. When he lets go, return the hose to the proper place to guide him back into heel position.

Saying Heel means for him to get back to heeling. Be sure you are telling Champ to do what you want of him.

While you're playing two hoses now, perfect his performance. If he is dropping the hose too early, before he returns close to you, hide the second hose from his view.

He knows this game by now. If he continues to drop it too far away from you, tell him Go Find It and make him go back and get the one he dropped. Continue the game as soon as he brings the hose closer.

If he's running past you without dropping his hose, tease him a little earlier with the second one. Assume a clear body posture that you are going to throw the second one, and tell him Out. Throw the second hose **as soon as** he complies.

Puppy Imprinting

A young puppy cannot heel. He does not have the coordination or concentration. He should not be expected to **learn** this exercise.

But you can make a positive *imprint* for this behavior. Teach the pup to take food from your hand and to look **up** at you.

With the puppy at your left side, teach him to walk with his head **up** a few steps. Feed him continuously as he walks with his head up.

Five or 10 steps are enough. That's about as long as a pup can be attentive. Use a clear, energetic release **before** he loses focus.

With a young dog, you may be able to repeat the 5 or 10 steps (with constant feeding) two or three times. Clearly release him from heeling each time **before** he gets bored or frustrated.

Remember that juveniles are often even **less** coordinated than puppies. Their growing bodies confound them at every corner.

Keep it short and simple and successful!

Patchwork

If your dog already knows how to heel in correct position, begin feeding him within the pattern after **every** turn, after **every** transition, and at **every** halt. Progress to using food as *motivation* to cement his **Attention** and improve his **Attitude.**

Be careful not to reinforce incorrect position. As he gets looser and happier, he may begin to forge or wrap. Steer him into correct heel position and feed him **only** when he maintains **Accuracy.**

With a dog trained originally through compulsion, it is doubtful you can change his **Attitude** totally. If he heels accurately, feed after every turn and at each halt.

Sits taught over compulsion are usually slow and stiff. Using food makes the dog faster and more relaxed. (See Chapter 7: The Solid Sit.)

Once the sit improves, begin using more food in heeling. Again, be sure to feed **only** when he is in correct position.

Using *play drive* constructively often goes a long way with this dog. Refer to the Play Drive section in this chapter. Teach him to play two hoses.

Guide his focus and **Attention** on the hose during heeling. (See Fig. 18, Page 108.) Let him bite the hose and play tug-of-war when he's correct. (See Fig. 19, Page 108.) Interrupt the exercises frequently by letting him bite the hose. Then play two hoses.

You may never totally rehabilitate this dog. But you can make training sessions a lot more **fun** for both of you.

Polishing: Teaches the dog that he must always pay **Attention** and hold correct position. Introduces consequences for disobedience. Improves intensity. Increases concentration and his desire to be **Accurate.**

20. HAPPY HEELING
WITH ATTENTION AND ACCURACY.

Introducing Corrections

When everything discussed to this point is finished, you are several months into your training program. The time frame depends on how often you train and your capabilities as a team.

The **Foundation** can't be hurried. We've taken as long as two years to complete the foundation, and it's always paid off in the end.

Before you begin your **Polishing** program, be sure of your understanding and timing. (See Chapter 4: Corrections.) Answer the questions posed there before proceeding.

Be absolutely certain you are correcting a **disobedience** and not a **mistake!**

Most corrections in heeling are for lack of **Attention** or incorrect position. After a solid **Foundation**, Champ knows exactly where he should be, how to get there, and that he gets what he wants as soon as he arrives.

His eyes should be on **you** and where **you** are going. **Attention** should be a habit by now.

Remember the basic rule: effective corrections work through the element of **surprise**, not pain.

At your home field, begin hooking the leash to both rings of the prong collar instead of the fur saver. Only extremely body sensitive dogs respond to corrections on the fur saver, but you can always try it first to find out.

Champ has been wearing both collars for **all** training sessions. He certainly won't make a collar association at this point.

From now on, be especially sure he wears his prong collar during **all** training. At the moment you need to give a correction, you can't go back to your training bag to get the collar!

Use your **first** correction for lack of **Attention**. Lack of attention occurs when the distraction is greater than the *motivation*.

Being distracted results in correction. Then we bring the dog back in *drive* and he gets his *reward* for being attentive again.

If your first correction is for position, the dog could move even further out of position if you really surprise him. That would prevent you from offering him instant *positive reinforcement* after the correction. And we want to teach him that something positive always follows a correction.

A correction almost always surprises the dog enough to look at you. Then you can reward **Attention** immediately, even if position isn't perfect.

At your home training field, when the dog looks away (more than a glance) during heeling, give him a **slight pop** on the collar and **immediately** feed him when he looks back. This first *imprint* of a correction must be to look for *motivation*.

This first introduction to a correction is not severe. When a dog is not already dulled to compulsion, he responds to a minimum of force. It **surprises** him. If he has not had a previous correction, the first one has a significant impact.

You can always correct harder in the future. But it is impossible to take back a correction that was too severe for your dog's *temperament*.

If he is looking down, on his way to sniffing the ground, the pop is **upwards**. If he is looking away from you, the pop is **toward** you.

This pop is quick and sudden. If done well, he doesn't even know where it came from. He looks to you to see if you felt it too!

You immediately feed him for his **Attention.** This teaches him to look for something positive after a correction.

This can become extremely important later, in case a stronger correction is necessary. The dog must learn to bounce back in *drive*. Remember the formula is

Drive − Force − Drive.

The pop surprises him. Then he immediately gets praised and rewarded for being back in **Attention**.

Your first correction tells you a lot about your dog and your training program. Evaluate this information before proceeding.

Corrections are needed only rarely for heeling, provided the **Foundation** is solid and the correction effective. If you give more than two per session, take time out to evaluate the situation.

After any correction, increase *motivation* and build *drive* again.

Once you are comfortable with your timing and your dog's response, you find that corrections play a very small part in this training program.

Remember that when done properly, corrections don't damage training, they should improve it.

But corrections applied improperly can damage your dog's attitude. They can confuse or depress him. This can make **you** an unfair pack leader and damage your trusting relationship with your dog.

Rely on motivational training first. It's safer and much more **fun**.

21. EXCELLENT ATTENTION
IN CORRECT HEEL POSITION.

22. DOG AND HANDLER IN SYNC AT FAST PACE.

23. A SOLID SIT WITH ATTENTION.

Chapter 7

The Solid Sit

*To a man the greatest blessing is individual
liberty; to a dog it is the last word in despair.*
                                    – William Lyons Phelps

Goal: To produce a square, solid, straight, relaxed sit done quickly. The dog's head comes up as he plants his rear firmly on the ground, with the dog's attention on the handler.

<u>Sit Position</u>

A correct sit is done front to back – nose to toes. The dog's head comes up, as he plants his rear **solidly** on the ground. This is done all in one fast, smooth motion.

Many dogs stop first and then sit from a stand, slowly lowering their rear ends and rocking back. This slow sit is often crooked, incorrect or incomplete (rear end not planted firmly).

In a straight sit, the dog's entire body (and all four feet) face the same direction as yours (Fig. 23). For a correct sit in heel position, his right shoulder is even with your left leg (Fig. 25, Page 122).

If the dog's shoulder is too far in front of the handler's leg, the sit is forged. When the dog's shoulder is behind the handler's knee, the dog is sitting too far back.

A true sit is so important that it cannot be emphasized enough. Many dogs do not plant their butts **firmly**. They are tense and stiff and their rears hover just above the ground, never actually completing the sit.

Champ should be sure and secure in the sitting position. He should sit quickly, all in one motion. He is relaxed, but still alert to you and ready to move (Fig. 23).

The sit is your basic position. It is the start and end of every movement. There is at least one sit, usually more, in each exercise.

Stabilize the correct sit. Make Champ consistent and comfortable in this position.

Foundation: Teaches the dog to raise his head while planting his rear firmly on the ground in correct position. Rewards every correct sit to produce speed and stability.

By the time you introduce a halt and have Champ sit, he is already heeling in correct position. When heel position is proper, the correct sit comes naturally when done quickly and smoothly.

Steer Champ into a proper sit with food in front of his nose. Prevent him from being out of position, just as you do in heeling. *Reward* **only** a correct sit.

Keep the food in your left hand, just in front of Champ's nose, as you are heeling and preparing to halt. Steer his head up and slightly back as you come to a stop.

Raise the food enough so his rear actually puts pressure on the ground (Figs. 24 & 25). Keep the food just above his nose, but low enough so his neck is not too stretched. Avoid keeping your hand too high, so he doesn't jump up or lift his rear.

The food steers Champ into correct position. Keeping the food just above and slightly in front of his nose (Fig. 24) prevents him from rocking back or rolling over onto one hip.

Feed **as soon as** position is correct. Hold Champ in this sit position for several seconds, feeding continually. Tell him Sit, Good Dog in a calm tone, each time you feed, to teach the word association.

Feed from your left hand, with Champ sitting at your left side. If using an entire hot dog, allow him to nibble it from the bottom of your hand (near your little finger).

<u>Body Position</u>

Keep your body posture correct. Stand up **straight** and keep Champ facing the same way you are.

You may have to use some body motion at first to help your dog sit straight, or to look at him to be sure he is correct. But quickly wean away from it.

Be sure both your feet are even and parallel, facing in the same direction. Avoid turning your upper body too much, even to see your dog's position. Learn to look out of the bottom of your eyes, with your head facing front. (See Fig. 23, Page 118 and Fig. 28, Page 130).

24. FEEDING CORRECTLY
KEEPS DOG'S HEAD UP.

25. CORRECT FEEDING
REINFORCES PROPER POSITION.

Stabilizing the Sit

Always hold **every** sit for several seconds. Count to five at least, feeding continually while Champ remains correct.

Releasing or moving off too quickly encourages an incomplete sit (butt not all the way down). When the dog is always ready to get up again right away, he doesn't relax.

Reinforce every correct sit with food. You make every sit correct because you steer Champ into the right position **before** he settles into the sit.

Avoid nagging your dog, telling him Sit, Sit, Sit. Be quiet as you guide him into position with the food. Once he sits properly, while feeding him, say Sit, Good Dog when he is calm and still.

This way he can concentrate and hear the command. We want him to associate the Sit command with being in the proper position, not **before** he sits or when he is half way down.

Feed **only** when your dog sits solidly. If he lifts his front feet off the ground to get the food, withhold it (by closing your hand) and lower it a little until he puts his front feet down. Then let him eat.

Feed **only** when he sits straight. If he swings his rear out, or rolls onto one hip, guide him into correct position with food. (His rear out to the left means you steer his nose further to the left so he gets straight.)

If he doesn't adjust properly, move forward a step or two. Use the food again to steer him straight **before** he sits. **After** he sits, *reward* and praise calmly with Sit, Good Dog.

Feed **only** when your dog sits correctly. If he is forged, withhold the food by closing your hand and take a step forward. Guide him with the food, keeping it back a bit further this time. Steer him into a sit where his shoulder lines up with your leg (Figs. 24 and 25).

If he's too far back, put your left hand where his nose **should** be and encourage him to move up into correct position for the food. If he doesn't, take a step forward and bring your left hand a little further forward this time.

When he does come up into correct position beside you, feed him. While he sits correctly, calmly tell him – Sit, Good Dog.

Food steering sounds **simple**. But it is not always **easy**. It takes practice to be able to steer your dog correctly and compensate for all his innovative actions.

Be patient and persistent. Champ gets better as your technique improves.

When Champ is heeling in correct position, a fast sit assures a correct sit. His head comes up and he plants his butt **before** he has time to get out of position.

Rewarding every sit with food assures that Champ sits quickly to get what he wants. Correcting the dog into a sit often produces a slow, tense sit.

Feeding him continuously at first while he sits assures a solid, stable sit. Correcting the dog to remain sitting often produces avoidance of the sit position.

Halt in the **same** place each time in the pattern. Thus Champ learns what to expect when. He is ready to sit properly and eager for his *reward*.

Get Champ's **Attention** before you halt. Stop only when he is watching you and ready to halt. This insures **Accuracy**.

Teach Champ to hold the sit position during praise (not petting yet). Tell him Sit, Good Dog, while he maintains correct position beside you. When he is solid, begin to lengthen the seconds between feeding while he sits, instead of feeding continuously. Keep reminding him Sit.

After many sits, as Champ becomes more secure and settled, teach him to hold the position while you stroke down his neck and shoulder. Be sure you have no food in your hand!

Petting is actually being used here as a distraction to teach Champ to remain sitting solidly. He should not move just because you do.

If you are not going to start or continue heeling from the sit, use your dynamic, energetic release after Champ has been sitting correctly for at least five seconds. Simultaneously, say Free and raise your arms up in the air to encourage him to leap up with energy and enthusiasm.

This release makes it **clear** to Champ that he is now free. He may not get up on his own, just because he thinks he has been sitting long enough.

He **must** remain sitting until you give him another command or release him. This is true of **every** command.

Begin good habits right at the start. This concept is especially important for the sit in motion, when you can only tell Champ to Sit once before you leave him.

After releasing, let him bite the hose and play tug-of-war. Or play two hoses for a few seconds if he has really done well.

Be careful not to wear him out if you plan to do any more training that session. Chasing the hoses saps energy quickly.

And remember not to play if that activity diminishes his *food drive* or makes his sit tense. We want to keep his concentration on the food for this exercise.

Play Drive

To use the *play drive* for sit, steer Champ into correct position with the hose in your left hand over his head (Fig. 27). Keep him there several seconds reminding him Sit.

Slowly lower the hose to just in front of his mouth, reminding him Sit. Then tell him Get It and let him bite the hose while he is in sit position.

Don't be concerned if he gets up or moves out of position while he tugs on the hose. He got what he wanted **while** in correct position.

As he gets more solid and secure, you can tell him Get It and let him jump up into the hose after he has held a correct sit for several seconds.

Using the *play drive* here requires a handler with great finesse, however. It also demands a dog with a calm attitude to concentrate on what he is doing while still focusing on the hose.

Food *motivation* is much easier to use and more constructive in this exercise, especially during **Foundation** work.

26. PUPPY SITS FOR FOOD.

27. PLAY DRIVE FOR SIT.

Puppy Imprinting

One of the first commands a puppy can learn is sit. Having the pup in front of you is usually easier than starting with him at your side.

Hold the food in front of his nose until he smells it and licks it. Then bring your hand up slightly and back until he sits (Fig. 26).

Calmly say Sit, Good Dog **while** he is sitting, not before he sits. Keep feeding him in position for two or three seconds.

Begin right away using an energetic, upward release. Even puppies learn this quickly.

Two or three sits at a time is the **most** you can do with a puppy. Quit while the work is still interesting for him and he still wants more food.

Be prepared for puppy antics. They usually jump and bite and invent a number of variations on sitting before landing in the desired position!

Even with a puppy, reward **only** a correct sit. Keep your hand closed on the food until he sits properly. Keep the food high enough to prevent the pup from rocking back or puppy sitting (flopping over onto one hip).

Refrain from saying Sit until the puppy is sitting correctly. We want the *imprint* of the word association to come for correct sit position, not for dancing around.

How the puppy sits these first few times is very important. This *imprint* lasts a lifetime and you want to make the **first** habit a good one.

A puppy is capable of sitting correctly for the food. So feed him **only** for a correct sit.

Once you teach the puppy to sit correctly, accept nothing less. Feed him only for a solid sit.

Remember that you can only **introduce** a puppy to the idea of sitting for food. He can not yet concentrate enough to actually **learn** the exercise.

Keep it short and simple – two or three sits at most. And don't expect him to do it on his own yet, without the luring and the *positive reinforcement.*

Patchwork

For the dog who is unsure, depressed or nervous from previous pressure training, feed him in **every** sit that is correct, even if it was slow. Show him the food as he starts to sit and feed as soon as he is sitting solidly in the proper position.

Force usually produces a slow, tense sit. In time, he may learn to relax and expect his *reward.* Steer him correctly and feed him **every** time he sits.

Keep reinforcing the correct sit. He sits faster when he relaxes and comes into *drive* with calmness and focus. This happens when he realizes he is not going to be corrected into the sit and you always give him time to relax into a solid sit.

Remember that retraining takes time. It often takes **twice** as long as the original training whipch produced the problem, and much longer than starting from scratch.

Polishing: Teaches the dog to bring his head slightly to the right and to focus on your face to give you his full **Attention** while still in correct position.

Teach the Attention Sit only after Champ consistently sits correctly within the **entire** heeling pattern. Also, the sit in motion should be stabilized first.

Begin with Champ in a correct sit and show him the food in your left hand. Bring the food **slowly** toward the

28. ATTENTION SIT.

center of your body so Champ's head follows. Feed him while his head is across your leg, provided his body is still straight and correct beside you.

Champ's head is now close to where it is during correct heeling (Fig. 28). The command for the Attention Sit is the same as Heel.

Stabilize this by repeating Heel, Good Dog. Feed him as he raises his head and turns to look at you. (Some handlers use a different command for this, such as Watch or Ready, but it is actually for proper Heel position.)

As Champ gets more comfortable cocking his head up and sideways while maintaining correct heel position, teach him to look into your face. Store some food in a top pocket.

With Champ's head in position toward you, reach up and take a piece of food from your top pocket as you softly say Heel. Slowly lower your hand with the food showing, keeping it in line between your eyes and his.

Feed Champ when he looks up into your face. Tell him Heel, Good Dog and feed as soon as he makes eye contact.

Teach Champ to hold this position by continually feeding him at first. Encourage him to raise his chin up even higher. But he should not touch your body or lean on you.

As he watches you longer, practice putting your arms at your side (Fig. 28) and then feeding him again. When he holds this position properly regardless of the position of your arms, progress to stroking the underside of his neck, from his throat to his jaw.

Return to feeding him whenever he maintains the correct position. Here again, petting is used as a distraction.

Champ must hold his sit position while you stroke his chin until his head is in the desired position.

Repeat Heel, Good Dog while petting him and bringing his head into the Attention Sit position. Avoid too much tension here or you incite his *opposition reflex*.

He soon comes to enjoy this stroking under the chin. Whenever he gives you his full **Attention** and looks into your face, while still sitting correctly, feed and praise.

Proofing

When Champ cocks his head and looks up at you every time you say Heel (quietly) and don't move, begin proofing by doing the Attention Sit near another person. Continue proofing until Champ keeps his **Attention** on you while another person walks past several feet away.

Reinforce with food **every** time he gives you his full attention. You are trying to convince Champ that **you** are the most interesting thing on the training field.

Remember that all proofing is done with *positive reinforcement* and *reward*, never with corrections.

Introducing Corrections

By the time you are proofing the sit, Champ is usually well along in the other exercises and nearly ready for competition. When you are alone on the field again, if your dog looks away while sitting at heel, you can give a quick pop on the prong collar.

This should **surprise** him enough to look at you. Keep your Heel command calm and quiet. Feed immediately after the correction, the moment he looks at you.

This pop is always done **toward** you. Feed him as soon as he responds correctly.

Correct **only** when you are alone on the field. Never correct while proofing or when you **first** add distractions.

Champ then associates the correction with the nearby people or distraction. He becomes worried and unsure rather than more attentive. He becomes confident only when he makes his own decision and then is rewarded for it.

Remember that proofing is **always** done with *positive reinforcement* and *reward*. We want Champ calm and confident in his work, even when there are distractions.

Introduce corrections without any distractions on the field. Allow Champ to make the proper association – that correction is for inappropriate behavior, not because of the distractions.

Once you are working on trial sequences, use the Attention Sit often and before each exercise. Reinforce **every** correct Attention Sit with food and praise.

The Attention Sit is useful on the competition field in many places. While checking in with the judge (and the other dog/handler team), you can now stroke Champ under his chin to be sure his head is in position.

This way you keep his **Attention** right from the start. You are sure he is not sniffing the ground or eyeing the other dog while you report to the judge. You don't want to lose him here, before you even begin your routine!

If your dog does look away just as you are ready to start an exercise, saying Heel brings him into attention. But more often, this training results in total **Attention** while Champ is sitting beside you so he is **always** ready for your next command.

29. ATTENTION SIT.

Chapter 8

Sit in Motion

All the virtues of Man,
without his vices.
— Lord Byron

Goal: To produce a fast, reliable sit on command. The dog's head comes up as he plants his rear firmly on the ground and remains in place.

Once Champ sits quickly and **solidly** in correct position at every halt in heeling (without steering), begin teaching the sit in motion.

Although you always practice the legs of the heeling pattern **shorter** than they are in trial, the build-ups for the motion exercises are one exception. Always heel **at least** 12 to 15 paces before commanding Sit.

Be especially aware of your tone of voice. Your Sit command needs to be light, with an upward inflection.
The command must sound very **different** from your Down and Stand commands. Your tone of voice must be consistent if your dog is to recognize and respond to this command while heeling.

```
┌─────────────────────────────────────────────────────────┐
│                SIT IN MOTION EXERCISE                     │
│                                                           │
│  From starting place on center line of field:             │
│        ● Begin in basic position (sit). Acknowledge judge.│
│        ● At least 10 paces normal heeling.                │
│        ● Command Sit as you continue walking.             │
│        ● Proceed 30 paces. Turn to face dog.              │
│        ● On judge's signal, return to right side of dog.  │
└─────────────────────────────────────────────────────────┘
```

Foundation: Teaches the dog to sit quickly immediately upon command, and to remain in place and wait for his *reward*.

When first teaching the sit in motion, begin with one heeling pattern instead of two. Return to your starting place.

Have food in your left hand. Tell Champ Sit and feed while he is in correct position.

Heel approximately 15 paces forward, feeding rhythmically when Champ is in correct position. Then put the food in your **left** hand just above and directly in front of Champ's nose to keep his head up and simultaneously stop his forward motion (Fig. 30).

Say Sit as you pivot directly in front of Champ (Fig. 31). You are now facing him.

Withhold the food in your left hand (still in front of his nose), guiding his head up and back, until he sits. Feed him the **moment** he sits (Fig. 31).

Practice your turn in front of Champ slowly at first. Spinning quickly might surprise him so much he moves out of position.

30. FOOD STOPS DOG'S MOTION.

31. PIVOT DIRECTLY IN FRONT.

32. FEED FROM FRONT
TO STABILIZE SIT POSITION.

33. STEP BACK BESIDE DOG.
FEED TO STABILIZE SIT POSITION.

As soon as he sits, feed him continuously (Fig. 32) from in front, telling him Sit, Good Dog. Still feeding him with your left hand, step back beside him and feed him a few more pieces in heel position, repeating Sit, Good Dog (Fig. 33).

Stand quietly for a few seconds and then clearly release Champ. Start again with him in the basic position (heading in the **same** direction down the field), telling him Sit and feeding from the left hand.

Saying Sit and feeding **before** you begin heeling establishes the sit at the start of the exercise and helps get Champ ready for what is to come. Normally you would say Heel (for Attention Sit) to get Champ in position to begin any other exercise. (See Attention Sit in Chapter 7.)

Start again, heeling **at least** 12 to 15 paces each time before the Sit command. Always keep feeding Champ on the build-up to prevent anticipation.

Practice this three or four times down the center line in the same direction in this session. As your technique gets smoother, Champ begins to get the idea.

End with heeling **all** the way down the center line (in the same direction as you did the moving sits), feeding rhythmically as you normally do in training. (See Chapter 6: Happy Heeling.) This helps prevent anticipation of the moving sit during heeling in your next training session.

Finish this heeling down the center line with a halt and correct sit. **Before** you halt, show Champ the food in your left hand and say Sit.

Feed him in correct position. Remind him Sit, Good Dog, while he is in position. This helps Champ remember the point of **this** training session and set him up for your **next** session.

Remember that when learning something new, it is especially important that Champ have his **quiet time** immediately after training. This helps him absorb his new lesson.

Stabilizing the Sit

The next few training sessions follow the same format as the first. Concentrate on stabilizing the motion sit as you turn **directly** in front of Champ.

Soon, he begins to sit **before** you complete your turn in front of him. When you see this, progress to taking one step past him before turning in front, then two.

Continue to use your **left** hand with food just in front of Champ's nose, however. Realize that he is still reacting more to your physical body cues than to your verbal command!

Once you are taking one or two steps past Champ, wean away from the physical cue of the food in front of his nose with your left hand. After you turn, however, **always** feed him from in front at this level.

Make Champ reach up and back for the food to keep the sit **solid**. Then step back to his side, feeding again from heel position (Fig. 33) before releasing.

The first time you drop the visual signal of the food in your left hand in front of Champ's nose with the command, he usually doesn't sit right away. He still responds more to the visual cue (body language) than the command right now.

You simply pivot **directly** in front of him, reminding him to Sit. Withhold the food over his nose until he sits. Then feed as you tell him Sit, Good Dog. As he starts to get it, make the transition from luring to *positive reinforcement* and then to *reward.*

No corrections at this point! He's still just learning. Allow him time to learn, without the stress of correction. He'll eventually catch on that his *reward* comes as soon as he sits when told.

Take your time with this exercise. Remember that it remains in the routine all the way through SchH. III and is one of the most botched exercises at that level! Build your **Foundation** slowly and correctly.

Going the Distance

Once Champ is doing this sit well, prepare him for your leaving. First do the sit in motion the way you taught it, pivoting **directly** in front and feeding.

While Champ is still sitting, remind him to Sit. Walk away, three or four steps in front of him, to be sure he is stable in the sitting position while you move.

Return to his right side and stand just slightly further back than heel position, facing in the same direction as Champ. Remind him to Sit, as you walk by him. Continue walking past him three or four paces.

Return again directly to his right side. (Be sure you **never** have food in your hand as you return or walk by.) Feed Champ in heel position.

After each sit in motion now, turn **directly** in front of him and feed right away. Practice leaving him a few more paces each time, after reminding him Sit.

Continue this exercise after each rewarded sit in motion. Champ becomes secure in knowing that you **will** return and feed him, even though you might walk away.

Progress to walking quickly past him while he is sitting. Say Sit as you pass by him. Then return to his **side** and feed him. As he gets more solid, extend the distance until you can walk 10 or 15 paces away.

Should your dog break the sit, lie down or get up, simply take him back to the **exact** spot you left him. Guide him into a sit with food and feed when he does.

Leave him only one or two steps. Shorten the distance until he is more secure.

Your dog breaks only when you progress too quickly. Avoid correcting him for your impatience.

Remember, you want Champ to be successful with each step. Progress slowly and **only** when he seems sure and secure in his sit.

Throughout these sessions, you still *reward* every initial sit with food. By now Champ is sitting reliably every time. Begin to extend the paces before you turn around.

Within the pattern, after 12 to 15 paces of motivational heeling, command Sit. Do not turn directly in front of him this time.

Take two more steps. Halt still facing **away** from Champ. Look back to see if he is sitting.

If he is, calmly tell him Sit, Good Dog. Return and feed

him in front as you continue to praise him. (If praise makes him break – you have not separated release and praise correctly.)

If he is not sitting, turn back and walk toward him as you command Sit. Feed him from in front once he sits.

We want Champ to believe that we turn within one or two strides of saying Sit. Then there is no reason for him to sit slowly or try to follow.

Once Champ is consistently sitting, even when you take one or two steps past him, combine the two elements.

Always turn within one or two strides after having Champ sit. Return and feed from the front.

Then leave again and practice walking by him (saying Sit as you pass by) and walking 10 to 20 paces away. Feed him when you return to his **side** the second time.

If at any time your dog does not sit quickly or surely, go back a step or two. Even if he is doing the exercise consistently well, every fourth or fifth time pivot directly in front of Champ, and feed him for sitting quickly.

If he isn't sitting **immediately**, return to pivoting directly in front and feeding for a few times. Continue until the fast sit is stabilized.

When the moving sit is consistently correct, incorporate it into the routine and walk a few steps past Champ. Do your two heeling patterns and then **one** sit in motion.

If it is less than perfect, take a little more time the **next** session to work on it. The sit in motion gets better and better as Champ begins to understand the exercise **within** the sequence of the routine.

Avoiding Anticipation

If the sit in motion produces anticipation or hesitation in heeling, simply offer **more** food for heeling during that part of the pattern. Remember that anticipation is the beginning of learning.

Encourage your dog to keep heeling by feeding him more, especially during the 12 or 15 paces of the build-up. We don't want to correct him for doing what we are trying to **teach** him right now!

Be glad that you are doing such a good job of teaching that he **wants** to do it. This means you are rewarding correctly and he understands the desired response.

In training, we always want to be sure that Champ is actually **learning** what we are trying to **teach**. Anticipation is one of the first signs of cooperation and understanding, even if he isn't doing it at exactly the right time.

Proofing

Once Champ is consistently quick and solid in the moving sit, you can add some distractions and temptations. These are designed to make sure he knows to sit and **stay** sitting.

First have another person observe your sit in motion. Without any body cues, command Champ Sit and walk five paces past him. Turn and face him.

Your observer tells you whether Champ was fast and sure on his sit. If he was, proceed with distraction training and proofing. If not, you have more **Foundation** work to complete.

Once an observer has assured you that Champ is sitting quickly and surely each time, that person becomes your distraction. Avoid using a person whom the dog knows too well or is expected to obey.

After leaving Champ on the sit in motion, have the other person walk around several feet away from him. If he is solid during this, the next session have them laugh, or whistle, or move quickly, or clap their hands, still a few feet away from him.

When Champ remains sitting solidly through the distraction, praise him with Good Dog, Sit. Then return to his side – praise, feed and release. Play a little if the distraction stressed or worried him at all.

Use only **one** distraction at each session. We want Champ to be successful so we can *reward* and praise him, not trick him into making a mistake.

Remember, this is **not** a time for correction. This is Show and Tell – Show Champ what's right and Tell him he's a Good Dog!

Polishing: Teaches concentration while sitting and rewards with higher *drive*.

Play Drive

Once you are including a full sit in motion occasionally into your routine, Champ is performing this exercise well. Food remains the best *reward* for this exercise throughout your training for SchH. I. After Champ is SchH. III, however, you can begin to *reward* in *play drive* if you want.

As you return to Champ from five paces away, remind him Sit as you take out the hose. (See Fig. 27, Page 127.) Stand beside him and remind him Sit, Sit as you lower the hose. Place it just in front of his mouth and tell him Get It.

Play tug-of-war here for a few seconds. Don't worry if Champ gets up from the sit **after** he bites the hose. He got his *reward* while still sitting.

Be careful not to let him get the hose if he breaks the sit or raises his butt, though. (Remind him Sit, Sit as you lower the hose.) His sit must be **solid** to get his *reward*.

If he responds well to this *motivation*, alternate between rewarding with the hose and food. **Always** make him hold correct position before rewarding.

Use the hose only one in four or five moving sits. Continue to *reward* with food most of the time.

To further polish the moving sit, you can incorporate it into your two-hose game. As Champ is near you, after dropping his hose and just before you throw the one you have, command him Sit. Be sure to use the correct light tone of voice.

If he doesn't comply, approach closer to him and repeat Sit. Refrain from shouting at him. Just repeat the command as you approach him.

145

As soon as he sits, remind him Sit and praise calmly. Go to his side and slowly place the hose just in front of his mouth, reminding him Sit. Tell him Get It and play a little tug-of-war. Then return to the two-hose game.

As Champ responds properly to this, you can progress to tossing the hose to him when he sits quickly and solidly and holds it for a few seconds. Be careful **always** to make him sit solidly for several seconds before rewarding him.

Do this very sparingly. Once or twice every 10 play sessions is quite enough. Remember that two hoses is a motivational game, not a time for nagging obedience.

This type of **Polishing** is done only rarely. It just helps Champ learn the technique of sitting promptly, even while he is moving quickly.

It cements his understanding of the command. It also builds his cooperation through *drive* and *reward*.

Introducing Corrections

Corrections for a missed sit in motion must be done tactfully. When the exercise is taught correctly (following **Foundation** training through all the sequences), it is almost always a **mistake** rather than a **disobedience.**

Confusion arises when we add the moving down and moving stands. Mistakes are usually from improper teaching, not enough **Foundation** work, inconsistent tone of voice, or simple confusion from the new commands.

The "famous Schutzhund III sit" (when the dog stands solidly instead), almost always occurs **after** teaching the stand.

This is usually a training or handling error and almost never willful disobedience from the dog.

Look closely at the dog's intentions before determining whether he deserves a correction.

Once the sit in motion is stable and consistent, you can correct Champ by showing him more clearly what you want.

By now you are walking two or three paces past Champ after you tell him Sit. (Every fourth or fifth time, however, pivot **directly** in front of him to remind him to sit quickly.)

If you turn around after a few paces and your dog is lying down, standing, or still moving, walk straight back into him. Walk slowly and calmly, without yelling or repeating the command.

While facing him, grasp his collar and ruff firmly with both hands – one on either side of his neck. Lift him up and back to place him into the sit position.

Once he is sitting, tell him Sit, Good Dog in your **normal** tone. No words are used **while** you are walking back to him or placing him in position.

Always make the correction **facing** him rather than **beside** him. This way he knows something went **wrong** with the exercise. We are not just starting over.

After you place him in a sit and tell him Sit, Good Dog, walk three or four feet away again. Return to his side and feed him as usual.

The next session, turn **directly** in front and prevent him from making a mistake. Chances are he will do it correctly the next time.

If your dog's sit is erratic, he probably doesn't really **understand** the command. Away from the training field, while he is free, say his name to get his attention and tell him Sit, using your usual tone of voice.

His reaction tells you whether he truly understands the command. Anything except an immediate, solid sit means there is more **Foundation** work needed.

Be sure understanding is complete before corrections are added.

34. SOLID SPHINX DOWN - BUT READY FOR RECALL.

Chapter 9

Dynamic Down

Dogs are not people dressed up in fur coats,
and to deny them their nature is to do them great harm.
– Jeanne Schinto

Goal: To produce a fast, reliable down on command, done all in one motion without moving forward.

<u>Down Position</u>

A correct down is done in one motion, with the dog rocking back (not forward) until his elbows are firmly on the ground. We strive for a down with the haunches upright and the dog's feet underneath him, called the Sphinx position (Fig. 34), rather than rolled over onto one hip.

Many dogs stop first and then lie down. Others sit first, and then lie down. Both techniques result in slow downs.

Dogs often do not like the down position because it is submissive. It makes them feel vulnerable. For these reasons, the motivational down is much quicker and more reliable than a down taught with correction, through dominance.

Your dog has no problem lying down in front of you to gnaw on a bone. You can use similar attraction to make Champ willing, even eager, to lie down on command.

Your tone of voice for the Down command is important. It must be very different from you Sit command.

Use a deeper, more authoritative tone of voice. Make your Down command serious, but not threatening.

Foundation: Teaches the dog to down quickly by dropping backwards to reach his *reward* and to remain until released.

When first teaching the down, begin with Champ standing (not sitting) near you. Show him food in your right hand just in front of his nose.

As soon as he shows interest in the food, close your hand. Lower it down and slightly back **all the way** to the ground as Champ's head follows it down.

The food arrives at the ground with Champ's head reaching back toward his elbows (Fig. 36), not forward toward his paws. If his rear is still in the air, use your left hand to stroke his spine, beginning just behind the withers.

Stroke his topline into the down position without using too much pressure, while allowing him to nibble the food to keep his head down. Trying to **push** the rear down only creates *opposition reflex* and resistance.

As soon as his entire body (elbows and hocks) reaches the ground, let him eat the food (Fig. 35). Keep feeding him **on the ground**, so his head reaches backward **behind** his front paws (Fig. 36).

While feeding, keep repeating Down. Keep him down with continuous feeding **on the ground** for several seconds.

Before he gets up on his own or rolls over onto one

35. STEER HEAD BACK WITH FOOD.

36. CONTINUE FEEDING TO STABILIZE DOWN POSITION.

hip, clearly release him. This release is an important part of this exercise. Your dog is **not** permitted to get up when **he** wants to, only when **you** tell him Free.

Be careful not to praise **after** the release. Praise comes **while** Champ is down, not when he is free.

151

Always teach the down from the standing position. Having the dog down from a sit forces him to go **forward** into the down by moving his front feet, which we want to avoid.

Once Champ is downing properly and consistently while standing still, incorporate it into the routine. Begin in the basic position (sitting in correct heel position beside you).

For now we are only teaching the down, not the recall. Calling your dog before the down is stable creates numerous problems.

During your 12 or 15 paces of build-up heeling, feed Champ rhythmically when he is in correct position. Here again, although you practice the legs in heeling **shorter** than they will be in a trial, the build-ups for the motion exercises are always **longer** than necessary to help prevent anticipation.

After at least 12 paces, when Champ is in correct heel position, use food in your right hand just in front of his nose to stop his forward movement. Command Down as you quickly lower the food **all the way** to the ground – directly in front of Champ's nose and between his front legs, toward his elbows (Fig. 37).

Allow Champ to eat the food **as soon as** his elbows and hocks reach the ground. The faster Champ goes down, the faster he gets the food.

Keep your hand on the ground, feeding continuously so he stays down. Be sure to feed **on** the ground (Fig. 37), not while his head is raised. Continue repeating Down to associate the word with correct position.

After a few seconds, release clearly. If your dog gets up

before you release him, guide him back down with the food. Repeat Down while feeding him there for a few seconds before you clearly release him. He must learn to remain down until another command or release from **you.**

Practice the down in motion three or four times down the center line in the same direction the first few sessions you introduce it. As your technique improves, Champ goes down faster and faster to get what he wants.

End with heeling **all** the way down the center line (in the same direction as you did the downs), feeding him rhythmically as you normally do in training. (See Chapter 6:

37. STEER DOG DOWN AND BACK FROM HEELING.

153

Happy Heeling.) This helps prevent anticipation of the down during heeling in your next training session.

Champ now gets his quiet time immediately after training. Remember that this time is much more important when he is learning something new.

Stabilizing the Down

The next few training sessions follow the same format as the first. Concentrate on stabilizing the down with your hand going to the ground as quickly as possible with the command.

Once Champ is comfortable going down and remaining for several seconds, begin to stand up **after** he is down. Continue to use the food directly on the ground to have him go down initially.

When he is down, feed him as you slowly stand up. Remind him Down as you toss food onto the ground between his front legs, toward his elbows. If he jumps up or snaps the food out of the air, go back to **placing** the food on the ground with your hand.

Once he stays down while you are standing, repeat Down and toss or place a piece of food on the ground. Remind him Down and take one step forward.

Turn to face Champ, reminding him Down. Place or toss another piece of food on the ground to keep him in position.

Continue this exercise until you can move two or three steps in front, returning to offer food after a few seconds.

Always *reward* with food on the ground between Champ's front legs (toward his elbows, not his paws). We want to encourage him to maintain his position and not move forward.

Stabilizing the down through *reward* takes a long time. Do not be in a hurry to add distance or test without food until Champ is going down quickly and remaining there willingly.

As he becomes more sure of the exercise within the routine, begin to lengthen the time between the command and rewarding with food.

Once you begin dropping the visual signal of putting your hand with the food to the ground, your dog usually doesn't down right away. His cue is still your body motion, not the verbal command.

Help him by offering **some** motion with your hand toward the ground. Praise and feed **as soon as** he downs completely.

When he is going down without any hand motion, command Down and halt one step ahead of him. When Champ downs, calmly praise and then return and feed him on the ground.

Going the Distance

Once Champ is going down without any hand motion toward the ground, prepare him for your leaving. For the first few times, go back to the way you first taught the down and use your hand with food on the ground as you command Down.

155

Schutzhund Obedience

When Champ is down, give him several pieces of food between his legs to keep him busy. Remind him Down and walk three or four steps in front of him. This demonstrates whether he is stable in down position.

Return **directly** to his side. (Going behind him only encourages him to turn and look and can make him move.)

Before you walk away from him again, toss a few more pieces of food between his legs. Repeat Down and walk away from him about three or four steps.

Turn and face him, repeating Down, Good Dog. Return in front and feed him on the ground.

Then return directly to his right side. Feed him on the ground again.

Stand up and wait for a few seconds. Then clearly release him just as he finishes eating the last piece of food. Keep him busy eating and he won't break position.

Continue this exercise after each down. *Reward* **every** down with food initially, as soon as Champ downs correctly.

Then progress to more distance away from him (up to 20 paces), returning to feed him on the ground. If he gets up or gets antsy and crawls forward, you have not yet stabilized the down enough to add distance.

Return to **Foundation** training sequences. Avoid correcting him just because of your impatience.

Proceed slowly and **only** when he is secure in the down. Make him successful in each step.

When Champ is downing consistently and quickly, begin to extend the paces before you turn around.

156

Within the pattern, after 15 paces of heeling (feeding rhythmically), command Down and take **one** more step. Halt facing **away** from Champ. Look back and see if he is down.

If he is, calmly tell him Down, Good Dog. Turn and feed him on the ground (from in front) as you continue to praise him.

If he is not down, turn back to him and place your closed hand with food on the ground where he **should** have downed. Let him eat the food when he downs correctly.

We want Champ to realize that the faster he downs, the sooner he gets fed. As he does this step correctly, add two or three more paces before you stop to look back.

If he moves forward before downing, or sits, or downs slowly, go back to feeding him immediately when you command Down. Remind him what's in it for **him**. Keep creating the correct habit.

As soon as the down is stable, do only one down per session within the pattern. **Always** practice it after the moving sit, in the same direction down the center line.

If your dog's down is less than perfect, go back a step and take a little more time on **Foundation** work the next training session.

The down improves as Champ learns what to expect. This happens when he understands the exercise **within** the sequence of the routine.

During all these sessions, keep the time Champ is actually lying down to about 10 seconds, except when you walk up to 20 paces away. Leaving him longer encourages him to roll over onto one hip rather than remain in the Sphinx position (on his haunches with both feet underneath).

When Champ is downing readily every time and is steady even when you are up to 20 paces away, add the come front. (See Chapter 11: Front to Finish.) You are ready to teach the front sit and finish some time before you are ready to add the full-length recall.

When Champ is consistently steady in the down position even when you walk 20 paces away and turn to face him, begin to prepare for the recall. (See Chapter 10: The Racing Recall.) Increase the time and distance you leave him. Add the recall from the down only after **Polishing** is complete.

Avoiding Anticipation

What happens if you get your dog so motivated that he starts anticipating the down or hesitating in heeling? Simply offer **more** food during that portion of heeling or in the build-up to keep him heeling properly.

Remember that anticipation is the beginning of learning. We don't want to correct him for trying to do what we're teaching him to do!

Encourage Champ to keep heeling simply by feeding him more during heeling. With the proper *motivation*, you can prevent anticipation and make your teamwork successful.

Proofing

Once Champ's down is fast and consistent on the command alone, you can add some distractions to be sure it is solid. Proofing encourages concentration and cements understanding.

First have another person observe your down in

motion. After at least 12 or 15 paces of build-up, command Down without any body cues.

Continue walking for five paces and then turn and face him. Your observer tells you if he was quick and solid on his down.

If he was, you can proceed with mild distractions. If not, more **Foundation** work needs to be done.

You become the distraction at first. Return to Champ and walk around him a few times, a few feet away from him.

If he stays down, praise with Good Dog, Down. Return and feed him on the ground. Praise and release. That's enough proofing for one session.

At a future session, take one of Champ's favorite objects with you – a toy, chew bone or the hose. After verifying that his down was fast and sure, stand a few paces to the **side.** (Standing in front facing him is not fair because he thinks it might be a recall.)

Take out the object and hold it so he sees it. If he stays in position, praise with Good Dog, Down. Put the object away. Return, praise and feed. Release clearly.

When Champ is really solid on his down, you can have a stranger repeat these distractions. But introduce them **slowly**. Use only one distraction per training session and proof only one in five sessions.

If at any time your dog creeps forward or gets up, **calmly** and **quietly** return to him. Say nothing.

While facing him, place two fingers in his collar. Take him back to the place he was down. Apply gentle but firm downward pressure as you command Down, not a jerk yet! (First use Show and Tell.) Feed on the ground **as soon as** he is down and repeat Down, Good Dog.

Repeat the distraction. When he stays down, calmly tell him Good Dog, Down immediately from where you are, so he knows he is right. (If your dog breaks position, you are not separating praise and release correctly.)

End the distraction so he knows he has done the right thing. Return to his side. Feed and praise, then release.

Remember that proofing is to make Champ more confident and secure that he is doing the right thing. He learns to concentrate and decide for himself.

The idea is to make him successful, not to trick him into making a mistake. Be conservative with your distractions and don't get carried away.

The point of these exercises is Show and Tell – Show Champ what is right and then Tell him Good Dog!

Puppy Imprinting

You can **introduce** a puppy to the motivational down. But don't expect any real concentration from a young dog.

Most important is to make the correct *imprint* so the pup knows how to get what he wants. You want his first downs to be done by dropping backwards, into a Sphinx position.

Kneel down or sit on the floor with a small puppy. Show him the food right in front of his nose as he is standing.

When he is licking and nibbling the food, close your

hand and slowly lower it to the ground between his front legs. (See Fig. 35, Page 151.) Feed the pup between his front legs, back toward his elbows (Fig. 36, Page 151).

Withhold the food in your hand until his rear is down too. If his rear doesn't go down, **stroke** down his spine, starting just behind the withers, to bring it down.

Be careful not to push down, just stroke firmly. Forcing the rear down on a young dog can do physical damage!

Some puppies resist going all the way down. That's fine. Then they don't get to eat the food hidden in your clenched hand.

A young dog must be **ready** to cooperate and willing to work for the food. If yours is not, then wait until he is. Try again tomorrow!

With a young pup who resists going down, it helps to practice on a smooth surface, such as linoleum. Their rear end tends to slide down when you stroke it, despite their efforts to keep it up in the air.

As soon as the puppy is down, give him the food on the ground (Fig. 35, Page 151). Keep repeating Down to help him make the word association.

Continue feeding for a few seconds to help stabilize the position (Fig. 36, Page 151). Then clearly release.

One or two downs is all a puppy can do. Don't push it, and don't rush it. Down will come when your young dog is ready.

Patchwork

For a dog who already knows down, but is slow or hesitant, teach correct technique using the method described.

Consider changing the command and retraining this dog. Learning may proceed more quickly and you may be able to erase a negative association.

If the dog was trained to down using compulsion, he may down quickly, but look pressured. Maintain the response, if it is fast and correct, but *reward* every down with food.

Over time, he may begin to respond more willingly, with less worry, as he learns he gets fed instead of corrected. *Reward* **only** if he downs properly, though.

Be careful not to encourage disobedience. Don't sacrifice control just to make your dog happy.

Remember that retraining takes time. You may have to compromise in the end and work toward training that is functional, according to his individual *imprint* and **Foundation.**

Polishing: Teaches the dog to remain down even when tempted through *drive* and how to down immediately even when moving quickly.

When Champ is fast and reliable in his moving down, and solid under distraction, you can switch drives occasionally. After you return to Champ's side, take out the hose.

Remind him Down as he sees the hose. Continue to remind him Down, Down as you lower the hose to just in front of his mouth. If he stays down, tell him Get It and let him bite the hose. Play tug-of-war with him.

This temptation through *drive* is especially important in preparing Champ for the recall. You want to be able to motivate him with the hose **before** doing a recall, but you don't want him to break the down.

To teach him to down at speed, use the down as you did the sit during the two-hose game. As Champ is streaking toward you, just after he drops his hose, command Down as you take a giant step toward him. Show him the hose you have instead of throwing it for him.

If he pauses but does not down, advance toward him reminding Down. When he does down, go immediately to his side.

Slowly lower the hose to just in front of his mouth while reminding him Down. When he is solid in the correct down position, tell him Get It and play tug-of-war. Continue with the two-hose game.

This game prepares Champ for the down while running in SchH. III and the down at the end of a flying voraus. Downs taught with *motivation* are faster and less resistant than those taught with compulsion.

Use the down sparingly during play, however. One down every four or five sessions of two hoses is quite enough.

Two hoses is Champ's game. It relieves his stress and makes him free. It is not a time for constant obedience or the purpose of this game is destroyed.

Introducing Corrections

After a few months of teaching and proofing the motivated down, Champ shows you that he understands the command. You can now begin to **insist** he always downs when you tell him.

The truth is, however, that by the time the motivational down has been taught correctly, the dogs rarely miss a down. They know they get what they want and eagerly throw themselves on the ground when they hear the command.

For dogs taught with these techniques, the down is not a submissive, vulnerable posture. It becomes a way to get what **they** want so they have no resentment.

However, should your dog not go down on command, simply return and face him. Say nothing.

Calmly reach for the double rings of the prong collar under his neck. Swiftly and surely correct him to the ground with a quick jerk downward and slightly back.

As soon as he is down, *reward* with food. Remind him Down and praise. Then clearly release and repeat the exercise.

If your dog has refused to go down on command even once, he **always** wears a six-inch tab attached to the double rings of the prong collar from now on. This is so you don't have to reach for the collar itself to make the correction.

If your dog has managed to move more than one or two feet from where you commanded him to down, calmly and quietly approach him from the front, saying nothing. Use the tab on the collar gently. Smoothly and quietly bring him to the **exact** location where you gave the Down command.

Once you reach the right place, correct him into the down with a sharp downward pop. When he is down, praise and feed.

Stand up and continue feeding him in that spot for a few seconds, reminding him Down, Good Dog. Clearly release and repeat the exercise.

For a dog who needs more than one or two such corrections for down, it is time to return to **Foundation** training until the down is stabilized. One of the steps may have been passed over a little too quickly, resulting in some confusion.

If your dog starts hesitating or failing to down once you begin to teach the stand, **help** him rather than correcting. Go back to Show and Tell – Show him what you want and Tell him he's a Good Dog.

This confusion is created by current training and is only temporary. It is just a learning phase. He is **trying** to do the right thing, but is unsure.

Help him and reassure him. After you have finished teaching the stand, the sit and down exercises come back correctly. Avoid adding to his confusion with correction. You only create anxiety.

Be sure to continue practicing the sit and down exercises while teaching the stand, but do them the way you did in **Foundation** training. Prevent mistakes and eventually the motion exercises come together in sequence for success.

38. A FOCUSED FRONT.

Chapter 10

Focused Front

An animal, especially a dog,
is possibly the purest experience you can have.
— Audrey Hepburn

Goal: To create a fast, close, straight sit centered in front of the handler. The dog raises his head to look up as he simultaneously plants his rear solidly on the ground.

A correct front sit is done the same way as the previously taught sits – front to back, nose to toes. Champ raises his head to look up as he plants his rear squarely and solidly.

When the dog slows and stops before lowering his rear into a sit, the front sit becomes slow. The dog also ends up too far away from the handler.

Ideally in the front sit, Champ looks up and focuses on your face (Fig. 38). This habit is created in the **Foundation.**

Foundation: Teaches the dog to sit straight and close and to look up into the handler's face as he sits.

Begin with Champ in the down position. Toss an extra couple of pieces of hot dog between his front feet to keep him busy.

As you remind him Down, take **one** step in front of Champ and turn to face him. Have two or three more pieces of food in your hands.

Just as he finishes eating the food on the ground and looks up at you, quietly and happily tell him Come. Show him the food in your hands held just in front of your body.

Guide Champ into the proper position by drawing your hands closer to your body (Fig. 39). Be sure to guide him in a straight line.

Raise your hands until the food is **just above** Champ's nose (Fig. 40). Be sure his butt is planted solidly on the ground. Give him the food when he is in the right position – close and square.

Keep your hands very close to your body. Encourage Champ to push his chest almost against your thighs and come in close to get the food (Fig. 41).

Lean **back** slightly (Fig. 42), not forward, to encourage him to come closer into you. Take a half step backward if he needs to be encouraged to come closer.

Let him eat the food **only** when he is correct. Keep your hands very close to your body and allow Champ to eat the food only when he sits close and straight (Figs. 41 & 42).

Lure him in with the food so he learns he must sit close. Avoid letting him sucker you into reaching out to feed him while he sits a few inches away. Teach him to push **into** you to get the food.

39. DRAW FOOD UP AND . . . →

40. . . . CLOSE TO YOUR BODY.

41. DRAW DOG IN CLOSE . . . →

42. . . . AS YOU LEAN BACK.

From the correct front sit position, always release backwards. This means you tell him Free and you move **back**, away from him, as you encourage him to leap upward.

With the release, encourage him to focus up and even jump up on you if he wants. This encourages him to come in even closer next time.

Three to five front sits at each session is enough. End with a correct front sit. End when you see Champ making progress and sitting closer and quicker.

While working on front sits, continue to reinforce the down with food on the ground. This avoids anticipation.

Prevent him from creeping forward by only taking **one** step away from him. Prevent anticipation by tossing an extra piece of hot dog or two between his front feet while you remind him Down.

Focusing on Your Face

As soon as Champ is holding his down and then springing up into front sit at your invitation, switch the focus from your hands to your face. Now teach him that the food comes from your mouth.

Guide him into a correct front sit with the food in your hands. Remind him Sit as you bring your hands up to your mouth.

Put a piece of food in your mouth (Fig. 43) and then let it drop so Champ can catch it (Fig. 44). This is easier said than done.

Spitting food (actually it's just dropping food from your mouth) so Champ can consistently catch it takes practice. You

43. DROP FOOD FROM MOUTH.

44. DOG CATCHES FOOD.

45. DOG WAITS FOR MORE FOOD.

may need to practice this specific talent **off** the training field until you and Champ perfect your timing and coordination.

If you miss your aim (or Champ misses a direct hit) and the food lands on the ground, try to catch his attention. Say his name and spit another piece of food right away, **before** he breaks position to get the one from the ground.

But don't correct him if he does go for it. Just try to avoid it by quickly using more food while he is in the correct position.

Be sure to *reward* Champ **only** when his front sit is correct – both straight and close. If your dog sits crooked, take one step back and guide him in straight with the food.

If he sits too far away, encourage him closer by patting your waist, lowering your chin and eyes, and backing up just a few inches. Lean **backwards** with your body (Fig. 42, Page 169). If he still does not sit close, return to guiding him with the food in your hands until he understands what you want.

As Champ becomes quicker and more consistent in correct front sit position, work on a few in a row. At first practice front sits from the down, so Champ learns the technique of leaping up quickly from that position.

Once his front sit is fast and correct, do two or three in a row. First feed him as soon as he is correct. Remind him Come, Good Dog and give him another piece of food. Then tell him Sit. Remind him Sit as you slowly take one step back. Then call Come in a light, happy tone of voice. *Reward* a correct sit and then release **backwards**.

Once Champ is consistently doing fast, correct front sits and is proficient at catching food from your mouth, you can back up **two** steps. Here again, offer more food on the down to prevent anticipation.

Be sure you stay in a straight line so Champ sits **straight** in front of you. We want Champ to be successful and get his *reward* so he knows where correct position is.

Practice front sits **only** from one or two paces in front of Champ. Going further away is counter-productive.

The front sit is not a recall. It is simply to teach correct front position.

We want Champ to dive into the front sit. When you go several steps away, it is not far enough for him to run, but it is too far for him to leap into position in one stride. So he trots or ambles in and then sits.

He sees he is going to have to stop in a few paces, so he doesn't use any speed. This is the exact opposite of what we want to teach. We always want a full power recall and a quick dive into front sit! (See Chapter 11: The Racing Recall).

Incorporate the front sit into each training session now. If the first one is perfect, *reward* and release. If not, then work on a few in a row.

After the release, turn Champ so he is facing down the field in the right direction. Have him down again (no build-up), using food between his feet. Then progress to a recall if he is ready. (See Chapter 11: The Racing Recall).

Begin adding the recall only after Champ is solid in the down. When he is waiting eagerly but calmly for your Come command, and then leaping up into front sit, you are ready to add the recall if he stays down calmly while you are far away.

Polishing: Teaches the dog to find the straight, close front sit and focus on your face, regardless of your position or movement.

Most polishing for front sit is done **off** the training field – in your yard or even in the house. Just before feeding is the ideal time.

Show Champ that you are putting food in your mouth. Work on a few front sits where you back up one or two paces. But do one or two at a **slight** angle. *Reward* (with food) every correct position (straight and close).

Ignore crooked sits. Try to encourage your dog to sit straighter or closer by slight upper body movements. If he does not sit correctly, however, simply do not give him the food and do it again.

At a separate session **off** the training field, teach Champ to ignore movements of your head and hands. Spit food to him as soon as he sits correctly. Then remind him Sit as you lift your head up and put your shoulders back so your posture is correct. (See Fig. 38, Page 166.)

Tell him Good Dog as he remains sitting in correct position, still looking at your face. Wait a second or two and then drop more food to him from your mouth.

Also teach Champ to remain in correct position as you move your hands up and down, in front and behind you.

Begin with **slow** movements. Remind him Sit as you do this. Praise him (verbally) when he remains focused on your face and then spit food to him.

If he should look away or look down as you move your head or hands, say his name and use your hand to point to your mouth. Remind him where his **focus** should be. Once his focus is on your face again – praise, *reward* and release (backwards).

As he begins to understand what you want, even with these distractions, gradually increase the time he sits looking into your face before you *reward* and release him. This builds his concentration and teaches him to hold the correct position.

When working on the training field in the pattern, give Champ the advantage. **Always** back up in a **straight** line from him. We want him to be successful here, not make mistakes that need to be fixed.

<u>Play Drive</u>

Using *play drive* to create even more intensity for front sit is easy. However, it should be done **only** after Champ's position has been stabilized with food.

Once he is fast and correct for food, switch to a hose occasionally. Show him the hose and hold it just above his head, but close to your body (Fig. 46, Page 176).

Slowly lower the hose as you remind Champ to Sit. Allow him to bite the hose while he is in position (Fig. 47).

Then release him and play tug-of-war (Fig. 48). This animates the front sit and increases focus.

Once Champ holds his front sit well, you can shift his

46. POSITION HOSE ABOVE
DOG'S HEAD IN FRONT SIT.

47. GIVE HOSE WHILE DOG
REMAINS IN CORRECT POSITION.

48. PLAY TUG-OF-WAR
AFTER RELEASING DOG.

focus up higher – to your face. Now place the hose under your chin.

Once he sits close and correct, remind him Sit. Slowly lower the hose to just above his head (Fig. 46) and let him Get It (Fig. 47).

If Champ waits **calmly** before you allow him to get the hose, you can progress to letting him Get It as you release it from under your chin (if you dare). But take care. Jumping up or wiggling back or barking are all bad habits created by the use of **too much** *play drive* for front sit.

Use the hose only one in every several sessions. Or use it just to bring back Champ's good attitude after a few sessions of working on angles or building his patience in waiting for his *reward.*

Again, three to five repetitions per session are quite enough. End with a correct front sit – praise, *reward* and release (backwards).

End each session when Champ shows even a slight understanding or makes just a little progress. But whenever the **first** one is perfect, end there.

Corrections

Front sit is **never** a place for corrections. Forcing your dog to be straighter or closer once he has arrived in front only creates avoidance of this place.

Corrections for front sit make the dog apprehensive and worried, so he slows down. Often, he avoids eye contact too and sits a little further away every time.

Make front sit **always** a most pleasant place for Champ to be. Show him how to get what **he** wants.

Reward his efforts to be correct and ignore any other behavior. This keeps Champ coming in fast and happy.

Proofing

Once **Polishing** is complete, Champ consistently arrives straight and close and focuses on your face. Now you can add a few distractions to the training field.

From the down, call Champ into a front sit from one step in front of him. Allow him to catch food from your mouth and then remind him Sit so he stays in position.

Have a person walk around several feet away. If Champ maintains focus and position – praise, *reward* and release backwards. No corrections here.

If your dog does look away, **quietly** say his name, point to your face to refocus him, and then praise, *reward* and release. Remember that proofing is done with *positive reinforcement*, reminders, encouragement and *reward*. This is Show and Tell time – Show him what you want and then Tell him he's a good dog.

When Champ is secure and focused while someone walks beside you, you can have them clap or talk. Keep these sounds quiet and calm, not aimed to startle or provoke Champ.

Every time he stays focused through a distraction – praise, *reward*, and release. Limit proofing to **only** one distraction per session, and only proof once every five or ten sessions.

178

Patchwork

For a previously trained dog who sits slowly, is crooked or too far out, or does not look up, simply *reward* **every** correct front sit. Teach him to catch food dropped from your mouth and **never** hassle him for being crooked or too far out.

Just do not *reward* these incorrect positions. Encourage him in or steer him into being straight. Then praise, *reward*, and release.

Over time, he may get faster and more focused when he finds he does not get corrected for front sit. However, realize that you cannot press "Rewind-Erase" and make him forget whatever happened to him before in this place.

Continue to **help** him be correct. But remember to forgive him his anxiety. It is probably justified.

Puppy Imprinting

The most important *imprint* for a puppy is to look up into your face. But to do this in front sit, the puppy ends up sitting too far away.

When showing a puppy, kneel down on the floor and lean you upper body **backwards**. First guide him into position with food from your hands.

Be especially careful that the puppy does not rock back to look up. Keep the food close to your body while feeding the puppy in correct position. **Always** release backwards by letting the puppy jump up on your chest.

A puppy can learn to look up into your face. Once the puppy knows to sit in front to get food, show him the food in your hand while you are kneeling. (Standing full height only encourages the smaller dog to rock back to look up.)

Then let him watch as you slowly raise the food to your face and put it in your mouth. **Immediately** take the food from your mouth and give it to him while the puppy is still sitting focusing on your face. One or two repetitions of this is enough.

But don't be surprised if this doesn't work yet with your puppy. Don't allow yourself to get frustrated. This comes in time, when your puppy is older.

And don't expect your young dog to catch the food yet. Few puppies or young dogs are coordinated enough to catch food consistently until they are older. Wait a few months.

If it does work, and the puppy starts to look up into your face, remember that we can only **introduce** puppies to the elements of some exercises. We cannot **train** them until they are more mature.

Even when Champ is old enough, perfecting the front sit takes time. But once he learns where his advantage lies, he flies into correct position and gazes adoringly into your face. (Is it you he adores, all those hot dogs, or his hose? Only **you** know for sure.)

Chapter 11

The Racing Recall

Dogs love company. They place it
first on their short list of needs.
– J.R. Ackerly

Goal: For the dog to come as fast as possible when called.

To teach Champ to come racing as fast as he can on a recall, the first step is to separate the recall from the front sit. Your dog learns to slow down if he expects to sit front every time.

The correct *imprint* for the recall is one of speed. Champ **wants** to get to you as quickly as possible. Then your responsibility is to keep him feeling that way!

Foundation: Teaches the dog to respond immediately to being called and run quickly all the way to the handler.

Teach Champ the Come command first. Have someone hold him by the collar (not the prong), or by a short tab (no leash on), at the same place on the training field you do the down in motion. They say nothing to the dog.

Show him the hose in your hand as you leave. **Run** to

DOWN WITH RECALL EXERCISE

From starting place on center line of field:
  For SchH. I and II:
    • Begin in basic position (sit). Acknowledge judge.
    • At least 10 paces normal heeling.
    • Command Down as you continue walking.
    • Proceed at least 30 paces. Turn to face dog.
    • On judge's signal, call dog.
    • After dog sits in front for a few seconds, finish dog.
  For SchH. III:
    • After 10 paces normal heeling, 10 paces fast heeling.
    • Command Down as you continue running 30 paces.

---

the **end** of the training field. Stand and face Champ. As you call Come in a loud, happy tone, the holder releases the dog.

Keep your posture erect. Stand up and show Champ the proper frontal body position for the recall.

Running backwards and clapping your hands, or kneeling down, may help him come faster now, but it will not work later in trial routine. The dog looks for those body signals and comes to depend on them. When he doesn't see them, he may slow down or become confused.

As Champ comes charging toward you, his ears are carried flat against his head if he is really running quickly. You stand still and say nothing. Just as he gets close to you, his ears come up.

At this moment, show Champ the hose in your hand. When he sees it, throw it **behind** you.

Stand still until he runs past you. Then, stay close to the same place and play two hoses for a few minutes.

One recall is enough for any training session. End the session with playing two hoses after the recall, but **only** near where you stood for the recall. This is developing important *place association* for Champ.

<u>Handling Notes</u>

Keep your body posture correct and your hands at your sides when practicing a recall. Alternate which side you throw the hose so your dog doesn't anticipate always going to one side or the other.

Throw the hose **behind** you, not to the side. Thus Champ expects to run past you and does not slow down.

Even if your dog comes slowly at first, not sure what to do, stand up straight and say nothing. When he gets close, show him the hose in your hand and throw it. He'll soon get the idea and speed up.

Always do recalls the **full** length of the field or further. Medium-length recalls only teach the dog not to use full speed. He learns he just has to slow down again when he reaches top speed, so he doesn't bother.

Five or 10 recalls with someone holding Champ is usually enough for him to learn the command and come flying to you to play. Keep it to **one** recall per training session, and use it as your last exercise.

<u>From the Down</u>

When Champ's down is solid even when you are far away, begin the recall from the down. Drop a few pieces of food between his front legs to keep him busy as you walk away. Take **off** his leash!

First, walk only a few steps before returning to drop a few more pieces of food between his legs. Once you have built high *motivation* for the recall, you have to keep the down position rewarding to avoid anticipation!

Return to Champ several times (to reinforce the down with food) while you are walking out to your recall spot. Turn to face him and be sure he looks solid on the down before calling him. If he is creeping, or picking his butt up off the ground, return and feed him more food more often.

Always return to reinforce the down once or twice before each recall. Every two or three recalls, return **all the way** from the end of the field, **after** you have turned to face Champ. Feed him while he is down and then leave again to do the recall.

Always *reward* the recall by playing two hoses. Keep Champ eager and excited to come to you.

Polishing: Teaches the dog to come all the way to you with speed.

Once Champ is racing to you on the recall, you want to focus him more on you. As he gets closer, hold your position just a little longer than you normally do before throwing the hose.

Now hold the hose just to the left or right of your body about waist high, and let Champ **jump** into it to bite it. (Be careful he doesn't bite your hands!) Then let it go and again play two hoses.

Be sure to hold the hose to the **side** of your body, or Champ might hit **you** at full speed. Alternate between the right and left sides so he doesn't learn to go to just one side.

Once Champ is consistently running full speed all the way in and looking directly at you for the hose, you can begin putting the recall and the front sit together sometimes. (See Chapter 18: Putting It All Together.)

Corrections

The recall is one exercise where there is no room for corrections. Keep Champ's speed fast and his **Attitude** happy by always giving him what **he** wants when he does what **you** want him to do.

Proofing

Once **Polishing** is complete, Champ consistently holds his down calmly, but is ready to run. He races all the way in on the recall and looks to you for his *reward*.

Before leaving Champ, toss him a few pieces of food on the down. Remind him Down and **show** him the hose in your hand to build his *motivation*. If he breaks, just keep the hose away from him. This obviously was **too much** attraction for his down.

Repeat, without attracting him so much with the hose. Feed him more between his front legs and leave again.

Then add one person walking near Champ's path while he does the recall. If he glances away, hold your position, but wave the hose and remind him Come in an excited voice.

You can repeat the exercise if he was distracted, but only **once**. Have the person stay further away from the dog's path and use plenty of play when your dog reaches you.

Once Champ takes no notice of a person walking near his path, you can add two people, or have one person walk a little closer. The people **never** interfere with Champ's straight recall, however.

If your dog gets distracted by any proofing, have the person back off and you add **more** *motivation* by waving the hose and throwing it a little earlier. One distraction is maximum per session.

Proofing is done only once in every 5 or 10 sessions. Remember, the aim of proofing is to make Champ more secure and confident, not to worry him.

Patchwork

For a dog with previous training who is slow or hesitant on the recall, simply *reward* **every** recall by playing. This dog needs **no** front sits here. He needs to learn that recalls are **always** fun.

Avoid helping this dog with extra commands or running backwards or clapping your hands. These signals may work in training, but they rarely carry over to the trial routine. When he doesn't see them, he slows down again.

Even when this dog comes slowly, throw the hose and play with him. Bringing his confidence back may take time, but your duty is to convince him that from now on **only** fun and play come at the end of a recall!

Puppy Imprinting

A puppy who already enjoys chasing the hoses (for brief periods only) can begin an *imprint* for the recall. Be sure he is energetic and ready to play, not well fed and sleepy.

Have someone hold the puppy as you **run** away in a straight line. They say nothing and ignore the puppy's squirming and protests.

You turn and face the puppy about 20 paces away (or further with an older dog). Again show the correct body posture by facing the puppy. Just as you call Come in a bright, happy tone, the holder releases your puppy.

As he races toward you, remain upright until he is about 10 feet away. Then quickly crouch down and open your arms to receive the puppy.

If he jumps on you, great. Let him knock you backwards and climb on your chest. Then play with him.

If the puppy doesn't jump on you, or looks hesitant at all, show him the hose and throw it a few feet **behind** you. Then play two hoses for a few tosses.

Three or four recalls, done correctly, (only one each time), make a lasting positive *imprint* on your puppy. Too many done too often become boring and counter-productive.

Remember that you can only **introduce** a puppy or young dog to an exercise. They are not capable of actually **learning** until they are physically and mentally mature.

One of the keys to a great recall is that Champ finds it **his** favorite exercise when it is **your** favorite exercise. Any disappointing training session can be ended with a **great** racing recall.

49. GUIDING DOG TO FINISH.

Chapter 12

Front to Finish

Yes, dogs can think.
(But) . . . they think like dogs.
– Jack Volhard

Goal: To produce a fast finish with the dog taking the shortest route around the handler and ending with a straight, square, solid sit in proper position.

Review correct sit position at the beginning of Chapter 7: The Solid Sit. A correct finish ends with Champ in this position – not forged or lagging or crooked.

The best finish is the one where Champ takes the **shortest** route around you. This is the fastest route, too.

We prefer the dog to finish by going **around** the back of the handler (Fig. 49), to his right side, ending in correct heel position. A swing finish, done totally to the left side of the handler, too often ends with a crooked sit or becomes incomplete toward the end of a trial routine when the dog is stressed or tired.

Begin the finish **only** when Champ is well on his way to being focused, intense, settled and steady in the front sit. Teaching the finish too early can lead to confusion.

189

50. SHOW FOOD.

51. GUIDE AROUND.

52. CHANGE HANDS
BEHIND YOUR BODY.

53. LEAVE RIGHT HAND
BEHIND YOUR BODY.

54. STEER INTO SIT.   55. FEED CORRECT SIT.

Teach the finish **separately** from the front sit. In the beginning, before the front sit is perfect and polished, always begin the finish by you stepping into front sit position rather than calling Champ into a front sit.

Foundation: Teaches the dog the technique of finding the shortest, closest, fastest way around the handler.

Begin with Champ sitting beside you. Remind him Sit and step in front of him. **You** move close to him so you have him in a perfect front sit (Fig. 50).

Have one or two pieces of food in each hand. Show him the food in your right hand (Fig. 50).

Tell Champ Heel and guide him around your right side

191

as he follows the food (Figs. 51 & 52). Your hands now meet behind your back, where you pass the food from your right hand to your left. Leave the right hand behind your back at first (Fig. 53).

Allow him to lick the piece of food in your left hand as you guide him around your left side (Fig. 53) into perfect position beside you (Fig. 54). Raise your left hand just above his nose and slightly back so he sits front to back here, nose to toes (Fig. 54).

Be sure you feel Champ licking the food or touching your left hand before moving it. Then guide him all the way around into heel position (Figs. 53 & 54).

You can remind him Sit when he reaches correct position. When he plants his rear **solidly** and squarely beside you in proper Heel position, feed him from your left hand (Fig. 55).

Handling Notes

Keep both your hands close to your body while teaching the finish. Then he learns to stay close to your body and not go wide.

Keep your hands high enough to keep Champ's head **up** as he goes around you. Moving with his head up makes Champ smoother and faster. He is also ready to sit faster when he arrives beside you.

Be sure to stop your left hand soon enough as you guide Champ into heel position for the sit. Allowing him to come too far forward results in a crooked or forged sit. It is difficult to back your dog up once he comes too far.

Teach the finish technique **slowly.** Champ will do it faster when he knows how.

Learning is easier when done slowly. Just because you learned to read slowly, doesn't mean you can't read fast now!

Reward Champ at first just for going around you, even if the finish sit is **slightly** crooked. Vow to perfect your steering next time. Once he gets the idea, and you steer better, his sit becomes correct.

Each time you practice a finish, be sure to give Champ a clear, pleasant Heel command **before** you move your right hand. You want him to finish on your command, not because of the movement from your hand.

With practice, Champ gets faster going around to get the food in your left hand. The technique is the same one you taught him for the about turn, so he picks it up more quickly this time.

Work on three to five finishes each session while teaching. Remind Champ to Sit and **you** step in front of him to begin each repetition. Once his front sits are perfect, you can **occasionally** finish from front sit.

However, keep the front sit and finish **separate** for most of your training. This prevents anticipation or crooked front sits because your dog is preparing to finish.

Practice finishes off the training field, too. Just before feeding, when Champ is really hungry, is one of the best times to channel this *drive.*

Once Champ gets the idea of how to finish, wean him from the movement of your right hand. Use less and less hand motion until he gets up and starts the finish without the hand movement.

Continue to use your **left** hand to steer him into a perfect sit beside you. *Reward* every correct sit.

If your dog is crooked or forged, withhold the food by closing your hand. You must have steered him wrong.

Remind him Sit, step in front (close to him), and repeat the finish. Be sure to give him a clear, calm command and steer him soon enough so he arrives in correct position sitting beside you.

Preventing Anticipation

If your dog ever attempts to finish before you give the Heel command, simply step back **quickly** to interrupt his way around you. Point to your face and remind him Come.

Reward the front sit with food. Make him wait a few extra seconds each time before commanding him to finish. Give him more food for the front sit.

With a dog who tends to anticipate, spit more food to him after you step into the front sit position. Doing this randomly **before** asking him to finish prevents the anticipation.

Finish is a fairly technical exercise for Champ. He must get up by himself, travel around you, and then find correct sit position in a new direction. All this he must learn to do without any movement or contact from you.

Give this exercise plenty of time and repetition before assuming Champ knows what to do. This is the most complicated technique you have taught him so far, so don't hurry it.

Polishing: Teaches the dog to find correct Heel position and come back into **Attention**.

A functional **Foundation** for finish can take months to perfect. Avoid polishing too early, before Champ really understands the technique and how to perform it consistently and quickly.

Polish the finish by adding the Attention Sit. Use this only after perfecting the Attention Sit as explained in the **Polishing** section of Chapter 7: The Solid Sit.

Play Drive

Using play for the finish usually gets a dog too excited and creates an unstable sit. The finish requires concentration and relaxation to be done absolutely correctly.

After a complete **Foundation** using food as both *motivation* and *reward*, switching occasionally to the hose can promote enthusiasm for the finish. But be very careful not to produce a tense, incomplete sit or wide, incorrect technique.

Show Champ the hose in front sit, and then make him wait a few seconds. Command him Heel and put the hose in your **left** hand as he comes around.

Hold the hose in the proper position on your left side as Champ finishes. (See Fig. 27, Page 127.) Remind him Sit as you slowly lower the hose into position just in front of his mouth.

Be sure Champ is still sitting squarely and solidly. Place the hose in his mouth as you tell him Get It.

Use *play drive* rarely and cautiously on the finish. Best to continue using food unless your dog really needs to be more motivated.

Puppy Imprinting

The finish is too technical an exercise for a puppy to grasp. Simple imprints like eating food from your hand, the sit and walking with his head up for food are the basic elements used later in the finish.

Proofing

Practice finishes on different surfaces, such as asphalt, gravel, dirt or concrete. When you are sure Champ has no problem with these surfaces, practice finishing where Champ has to change footing as he goes behind you.

Practice finishes while someone stands several feet away. Put a leash on for this, just in case he decides to go visiting.

The leash is to **prevent** him from leaving, not to correct him. Make him want to stay with you by making yourself more interesting and offering more *reward* when Champ is correct.

Once he ignores anyone around you, they can walk

around, clap or talk. Every time he concentrates on finishing instead of checking out the distraction – praise and *reward* with several pieces of food while Champ is in correct position. Then release.

Use distractions sparingly, only once during a session and only once in every 5 or 10 training sessions. Remember that proofing is to make Champ successful and thus build his confidence, **not** to trick him into making a mistake so you can correct him.

Corrections

The only really productive correction used on the finish is for the Attention Sit. This is done only **after** the dog fully understands the Attention Sit.

If he completes the finish, but looks away or gets distracted, a quick pop on the prong collar brings him back into **Attention**. Then *reward* with food.

Thus each exercise eventually ends exactly the same way it begins, with Champ giving you his full **Attention** in the correct basic position.

A proper finish is the perfect ending to several exercises, including all recalls and retrieves. It leaves the judge with a pleasing picture.

Perfecting the finish is not difficult, but it does take time. Teaching a perfect fluid finish in the beginning is well worth your time and effort, so be patient.

56. A FUTURE HAPPY RETRIEVER.

Chapter 13

Rocket Retrieves

He was one of these dogs
that will play fetch forever.
– Bill Murray

Goal: To produce a fast retrieve, going out and back as fast as possible, with a quick pick-up, a firm grip on the dumbbell, and a close, correct presentation in front sit.

Teaching a dog to retrieve the dumbbell as fast as he can is not an easy task, as anyone who has ever watched a Schutzhund trial can testify. Many dogs fly out **after** the thrown object, but their way **back** rarely rivals their top speed.

Champ should fly back with the dumbbell as fast as he goes out. He should dive into front sit, eager to be there and present his prize to you.

The general lack of enthusiasm most dogs have for the dumbbell can be attributed to improper **Foundation**. For Champ to be a consistently happy, fast retriever, he must love the dumbbell and **want** to bring it to you.

Some force retrieve methods apply compulsion even before the dog knows how to avoid it. This way the dumbbell

---

RETRIEVE EXERCISE

Facing away from the jumps:
- Begin in basic position (sit). Acknowledge judge.
- Throw the dumbbell at least 10 paces.
- After the dumbbell stops rolling, command Fetch (Brings).
- Stand still until dog presents dumbbell in front.
- Command Out and take dumbbell.
- Place dumbbell at your right side.
- Command Heel.
- Exercise is complete when dog is back in basic position.

SchH. I uses 650 gram dumbbell.
SchH. II uses one kilogram dumbbell.
SchH. III uses two kilogram dumbbell.

---

creates a most unpleasant *imprint* for the dog.

Some methods use force while the dog is returning, or to create the front sit. These actions then become extremely unpleasant for the dog.

Consequently, we see pressure and conflict (or avoidance) on these parts of the exercise. For some dogs, their **Attitude** to retrieving the dumbbell is forever broken.

The answer is to build a motivational **Foundation.** When Champ enjoys his dumbbell work, and wants to play the game with **you**, he has a good *imprint*. Then we are on our way to full points in this exercise.

Foundation: Channels the dog's *prey drive, play drive* and *fight drive* into desire for the dumbbell and enthusiasm for retrieving and bringing it back to the handler.

The best way to begin is with two people. You bring Champ out on a six-foot leash attached to the dead ring of his fur saver collar.

The second person tosses and kicks the dumbbell around (just out of Champ's reach) and **teases** him with it. Once Champ shows a strong desire to bite it, the teaser holds the dumbbell by the bells, just off the ground, and allows him to bite the bar.

The first few times, Champ wins the dumbbell immediately when he grips the bar. You praise Champ (verbally with Fetch, Good Dog) while running **quickly** in a circle to encourage him to hold and carry the dumbbell.

Sound familiar? Yes, we want to spark the same drives here as are activated in carrying the protection sleeve calmly and firmly. So these techniques seem similar to those some use in beginning bitework.

When Champ is gripping the dumbbell well, the teaser plays tug-of-war and wrestles with the dumbbell. You **always** keep the leash constantly taught while he is tugging, thus allowing the teaser to keep **tension** between himself and Champ with the dumbbell in the middle.

Progress to letting Champ win **only** when he has a full, firm, hard grip on the dumbbell, holding it just behind his canines.

Remember that producing *drive* means creating calm focus, then you *reward* this concentration. Avoid creating hectic behavior.

Pushy Presentation

As Champ circles, you slowly guide him toward you as you back away, using gentle pops on the leash. Pulling only creates *opposition reflex*. Now **you** begin to make him want to play with you with the dumbbell.

Touch the dumbbell, but only for an instant. Champ wins, but only for a moment. Touch the bells again quickly, but briefly, before Champ can turn away from you.

Tap the sides of the dumbbell, pushing it gently **away** from you, as you keep backing up. This incites Champ's *opposition reflex*, encouraging him to push the dumbbell **toward** you instead of pulling away. Take care that Champ perceives that he always wins this game.

Once Champ starts coming to you to play, grab the dumbbell briefly. Let go instantly, so Champ gets it. Praise and repeat Fetch whenever Champ wins.

But grasp the bells again **quickly** each time before he turns away so much that you can't reach him again. Do this two to four times each time Champ has the dumbbell before letting him carry it again.

Champ wins for a moment each time. Always move **backwards** as you play "push-away" to encourage him to come after you.

Resist chasing him, reaching too far for the dumbbell or grabbing it for too long. Make him **want** to bring you his prize to play and fight.

If your dog does manage to turn away from you, simply trot off in another small circle, praising him all the time with Fetch, Good Dog. If he drops the dumbbell at any time, immediately tighten the leash so he **cannot** reach it.

Restrain your dog while you kick the dumbbell away, back to the other person. This makes him **want** to keep and carry the dumbbell next time, just as kicking the sleeve away in protection makes him want to chase and keep that.

After only a few repetitions, run Champ off the field carrying the dumbbell. Run quickly so he doesn't drop it.

If he does drop it, tighten the leash and **prevent** him from picking it up again. Hold him tight and kick the dumbbell away. Let him watch it roll for a few seconds, and then run him out without saying anything.

Praise for retrieving work **always** comes **while** Champ has the dumbbell in his mouth. Be careful not to praise **after** he has released it.

If he carries it all the way out, continue trotting around as long as he holds it. Or play "push-away" if he wants to fight with you.

When he does drop it, kick it away to make him want it next time. Or you can have someone **steal** it away to build even more desire.

If you are lucky enough to have one of those tremendously object-obsessive dogs who won't drop the dumbbell, have him out it for food or a hose. Then kick the dumbbell away and don't let him get it to build *drive* for the next session.

Keep dumbbell sessions short. End while he still wants more. If your dog has the drives needed for the sport, and you are activating them properly, he shows a strong desire to grip and carry the dumbbell after a few such sessions.

When Champ shows he really **wants** the dumbbell, the teaser starts holding it by the bells **on** the ground instead of just above. This teaches the technique of picking it up from the ground.

The teaser **always** still holds the dumbbell horizontal, by both bells, to force Champ to pick it up by the bar. This creates a proper *imprint.*

Once Champ is coming back to the handler joyfully to play "push-away," and his desire for the dumbbell is intense, progress to a little tug-of-war with the dumbbell instead of just pushing it away.

At this point, you can probably start playing the game by yourself. Hold the leash tight (to create *opposition reflex*). Tease him with the dumbbell and hold it just out of his reach.

When you see he **really** wants the dumbbell, allow him to snatch it out of your hand with a firm grip. Hold the dumbbell horizontal, by the bell, so he **has** to grip the bar.

Back up and encourage him to come in close and push the dumbbell **into** you. Allow him to initiate "push-away" or tug-of-war and then you always respond.

Keep dumbbell sessions **short.** Load Champ with concentrated *drive* for the dumbbell (not hectic action). Then leave him at his highest peak. Stop while he still wants more.

Even if your dog does not like this game at first, persevere. Keep **your** attitude excited and enthusiastic.

Chances are your dog will eventually **want** to play this game when he sees **you** are having so much fun.

Remember not to allow negative emotions to enter your training. This introduction still produces a positive *imprint* and proper **Foundation**.

No matter what happens, you can always finish with a force method, so your dog **can** learn to retrieve even if he has less *drive*. However, teaching him to enjoy retrieving is much more rewarding in the long run for both you and your dog!

Close Sit

Champ's front sit **must** be solid and secure before attempting it with the dumbbell. When Champ is consistently snatching the dumbbell and pushing it into you to play, gradually add the front sit.

As he pushes the dumbbell into you, calmly ask him to Sit. Back up a step or two if he rocks back or moves away.

Even if he **starts** to sit, play tug-of-war for a second and then let Champ win. When he always wins, he wants to come back for more, especially when you **push** the dumbbell back into him instead of taking it away from him.

Continue asking for a more solid sit, calmly repeating Sit, Sit, as he pushes into you. When Champ sits, grab the dumbbell and play tug-of-war. But let him win instantly.

To avoid mouthing, keep your dog busy while the dumbbell is in his mouth. Keep the time short, only a few seconds, that the dumbbell is in his mouth without your pressure on it for tug-of-war or "push-away."

When Champ is returning eagerly and sitting in front when you ask, command Out. The moment he gives up the dumbbell, let him jump up and grab it to play tug-of-war again.

Avoid pulling the dumbbell out of his mouth or fighting him to out. Put no pressure on the dumbbell. Hold the bells gently, waiting for him to **give** it to you.

Alternate between Out and playing tug-of-war when your have Champ sit in front. Keep playing "push-away" too, to encourage him to keep coming in fast and close and pushing **into** you. Add the front sit only occasionally.

Once he sits front consistently when you ask him, pushing the dumbbell into you and outing on command, add a food *reward* occasionally. Tell him Out, drop food to him from your mouth, and then let him jump up and grab the dumbbell again for tug-of-war.

Always end with a little teasing to establish *drive* for the next training session. When you take the dumbbell away from Champ for the last time, allow him to jump for it as you snatch it just out of his reach so he can't get it.

The Pick-Up

When Champ is doing this well, taking the dumbbell out of your hand consistently and then pushing it into you to fight and play, teach him to pick it up off the ground. Build his desire for the dumbbell by teasing, and then toss it just a few feet away

Keep leash tension to create *opposition reflex* and build Champ's desire to get to his dumbbell. Keep the leash tight so he can't pick it up until it has **stopped** moving. Sending a dog to get a rolling dumbbell encourages him to grasp the bell (not the bar), or to stop it with his feet.

Allow him to **drag** you to the dumbbell to get it. Praise lavishly when he does with Fetch, Good Dog.

Again, if he does not immediately come back to you to play "push-away," back up as you run him in a small circle. Encourage him to bring it to you to fight and play.

Faster Finish

Only **after** Champ's finish is fast and solid do you add it to the retrieve. Once Champ is snatching the dumbbell off the ground, turning to push it into you, and sitting and outing sometimes, you can **occasionally** add a finish.

When you do, place the dumbbell at your right side after the out. Shield it with your hand and wrist. After building so much desire for the dumbbell in training, we don't want him snatching it on his way by.

When he arrives in correct heel position, **slowly** bring the dumbbell **behind** your back into position just above his head, reminding him Sit. Release him with Get It and allow him to grab the dumbbell for tug-of-war again.

Even though Champ may do this very well, add the finish to retrieving only **rarely**. Once in every five training sessions is quite enough.

The Question of Force

By now Champ has all the functional elements of a retrieve. He loves his dumbbell and wants **you** to play or fight with him with it. Champ has a positive *imprint* for this exercise.

Only now do you need to make the decision of whether to use force to finish the retrieve. Many dogs with high *drive* can learn to retrieve reliably through a proper motivational **Foundation**, but it takes time and energy.

Should you decide on a force retrieve, there are several options. Whichever one you choose, Champ's love for the dumbbell created through this type of **Foundation** usually carries over, provided the compulsion is applied properly.

Just remember that training any force retrieve properly usually requires **many** weeks of consistent progression for the dog to understand completely how to avoid the force. (This is a book in itself.)

Once you introduce force, do not revert to playing with the dumbbell until the retrieve is finished. Then you can return to allowing your dog to be pushy with the dumbbell.

Do not be too eager to resort to force, however. Done incorrectly, it can break down your dog's retrieve.

Take lots of time to build Champ's *drive* for the dumbbell. He may surprise you with how reliable his retrieving can be.

Polishing: Teaches the dog to fly out and come back even faster with the dumbbell.

Once Champ is eager and enthusiastic to pick up the dumbbell, use his *opposition reflex* to build even more *drive*. Begin with him beside you.

Have the dumbbell in your right hand. Slip two fingers of your left hand through Champ's fur saver to **prevent** him from leaving your side. Throw the dumbbell, but not too far.

Use tension on Champ's collar to incite his *opposition reflex*. Keep him there only a second or two before releasing his collar as you tell him to Fetch.

Repeat this procedure once or twice each dumbbell session, until making Champ wait creates even more energy and enthusiasm to go get the dumbbell. Then begin extending the time you hold him, to three or four seconds, before allowing him to go.

When his retrieve is fast and reliable, teach him that he must **sit** and wait until allowed to retrieve. Have him sit beside you as you toss the dumbbell.

After the dumbbell lands, make Champ sit (no tension on the collar) and feed him there. When he is calm and concentrated, send him to retrieve.

Once he masters this, progress to using a tab on his fur saver collar. Simply hold the tab in your left hand (with no pressure) while you throw the dumbbell.

If your dog breaks too early, the tab stops him. You say nothing. Simply remind him to Heel and feed when he is back in position. As soon as he settles, send him to retrieve.

When he sits and waits consistently, even if only for a few seconds, return to holding the collar every few retrieves to bring him back in *drive*.

If any of the above progressions create confusion or hesitation in your dog, return to holding him by his collar until he is more sure at that level. Avoid sacrificing *drive* for control at this point.

57. ATTENTION SIT
BEFORE RETRIEVE.

58. TUG-OF-WAR WITH DUMBBELL.

When Champ is waiting eagerly, but solidly, for your command, you can polish the exercise even further by insisting on an Attention Sit. After throwing the dumbbell, simply have Champ look at you (Fig. 57), using the Heel command. (See **Polishing** in Chapter 7: The Solid Sit.) Allow him to retrieve the moment he looks at you in full **Attention.**

As Champ learns to wait for your command to retrieve, you can also be teaching him to hurry back even faster to **push** the dumbbell into you to play and fight. You can progress to letting him **jump** into you to play.

Use your hands as a signal. As Champ returns with the dumbbell, back up and raise your open hands slightly. Hold them open so that when he arrives, he pushes the dumbbell right into your hands for tug-of-war (Fig. 58).

Gradually raise your hands so Champ learns to **jump** up into your hands so you can grab the dumbbell. Then play tug-of-war.

Alternate between letting him win, or then having him sit and out, only to let him jump up and play tug-of-war again. Be sure he comes to front sit when you don't invite him to play. Practice a full retrieve with proper body posture and hand position (at your sides) once every few sessions.

Puppy Imprinting

Retrieving is natural for the true working dog. Learning to play the two-hose game is the best *imprint* for a young dog.

This game teaches a quick strike and pick-up. It also teaches the young dog to come back quickly to play again.

Use caution here. Stop while the young dog is still **high** in *drive* and wants more.

Remember you can only **introduce** a young dog to these activities. Going on just a little too long results in boredom and can destroy *drive* instead of build it.

Patchwork

For a dog whose **Attitude** for retrieving has been broken, there is very little that has been proven successful. These dogs are usually depressed about the dumbbell because too much force, or incorrect force, was used during **Foundation.** Their lasting *imprint* remains negative.

You can often teach these dogs to do an individual retrieve happily, with much time and energy. But this often does not transfer and breaks down within the routine. There they become worried and slow again.

The best patchwork for slow retrieving is simply to feed or play **every** time the dog returns with the dumbbell. Expecting something pleasant may, in time, change his mind.

Although this dog isn't flashy, he's usually reliable. You can't always make this dog fast and happy, but sometimes you can ease his pressure and pain.

A dog who loves to retrieve and play when running loose should be a happy retriever on the field. Building a **Foundation** through *drive* helps ensure his love of retrieving throughout his career and makes for an impressive picture on the trial field.

59. PLAYING/FIGHTING WITH DUMBBELL.

60. UP AND OVER THE WALL.

Chapter 14

Up and Over

It seemed the ordained order
of things that dogs should work.
— Jack London

Goal: To produce a dog who jumps cleanly and correctly with confidence, over and back reliably on one command.

For a dog to jump with confidence, he must learn the correct technique. Most dogs can get themselves over an obstacle in their own way, but to enjoy jumping a hurdle he can more easily go around, Champ needs to learn **how**.

Jumping is an athletic exercise. Your dog needs to be physically mature and in good condition before you start to teach jumping.

Your dog must not be overweight. **Always** do some heeling or play two hoses before jumping to warm up Champ's muscles.

Before jumping your dog, have your veterinarian confirm that he is physically sound. A dog should never jump more than his height at the withers until his hip X-ray verifies his ability to perform such activities.

JUMPING EXERCISES

Facing the jump a reasonable distance away:
- Begin in basic position (sit). Acknowledge judge.
- Throw dumbbell a reasonable distance over the jump.
- Command Hup.
- When dog is over jump, command Fetch or Brings.
- Stand still until dog presents dumbbell in front.
- Command Out and take dumbbell.
- Place dumbbell at your right side.
- Command Heel.
- Exercise is complete when dog is back in basic position.

SchH. I, II and III use 650 gram dumbbell over hurdle and wall.

If your dog refuses to jump at any time during training, or wants to step on the jump to get over, consider physical limitations **first.** Back, shoulder and stifle problems are often responsible for dogs refusing or hesitating to jump.

Never force a dog to jump if he is lame, stiff or sore. A physically healthy dog rarely refuses to jump when he has learned how. Most dogs actually enjoy it when taught properly.

Correct jumping technique involves Champ using his rear end to thrust himself over in an arc (Fig. 65, Page 227). Proper jumping demands a lot of rear end action.

Your dog needs to generate height, not width and speed, to jump properly. Allowing him to hurl himself at the hurdle from several feet away is a prescription for disaster.

61. TEACH CORRECT TECHNIQUE
BY APPROACHING JUMP SLOWLY.

Foundation: Teaches the dog to jump by using correct technique.

Begin introducing the jump once Champ has been heeling correctly for several weeks. Set the jump to approximately the height of your dog's withers.

Attach a four to six-foot leash to the **dead** ring of Champ's fur saver collar. No chokers here, please!

Heel Champ straight toward the jump. As you approach the **base** of the jump, when you are just a few feet away, command Champ Hup and allow the leash to go **slack** (Fig. 61).

Trying to jerk or pull your dog over the jump only creates *opposition reflex* and interferes with his concentration. Leave the leash loose and allow him to think about the task at hand.

You pass just to the right of the jump as Champ goes over (Fig. 61). On the other side, invite Champ to Heel again in a straight line away from the jump.

Introducing the jump this way creates a calm attitude and allows Champ to think about technique. It also encourages him to use his rear end to thrust over the jump because he is not moving with any speed.

After an about turn, repeat the same approach to the jump in the other direction. Heel away again in a straight line on the other side and then release Champ.

If your dog has any hesitation about jumping, lower the hurdle slightly and you **step** over it with him for the first few times. Once he is jumping consistently on Hup, start passing to the side of the jump instead of stepping over.

Repeat this procedure several times each training session until Champ gathers himself and jumps with energy and enthusiasm from near the base of the jump. He should seem confident, but calm, about the entire activity.

Keep him in heel position all the way to the jump.

Discourage any attempt to hurl himself at the jump or leave the ground too far back.

The exception is when your dog has any sort of minor disability. (Dogs with major disabilities should not be asked to jump.)

A dog with some physical limitations may need to generate more speed to help himself get over the jump. Allow him to approach the jump at a slightly faster pace and add a little *motivation*, such as throwing the hose **after** he lands on the other side, to help him enjoy jumping.

Once Champ is jumping properly by your side, teach him to jump by himself. Now allow him to jump **ahead** of you when you give the Hup command.

Continue to go to the other side and heel him away in a straight line and then release. When he does this properly, begin raising the height of the jump.

Keeping the jump too low, for too long, creates lazy habits. When Champ is jumping consistently on command, raise the height to about 30 inches.

Raise the jump to full height (39 inches) about once about every five training sessions during teaching. Jump full height **only** when Champ is in good *condition* and completely warmed up.

Polishing: Teaches the dog to jump from any angle.

To perfect Champ's understanding that he **must** jump, teach him to go over the hurdle from any angle. This can easily be necessary when the dumbbell rolls off to one side.

219

Sit Champ **slightly** off center facing the jump. Keep the jump at withers height for this training and place him **one** stride away.

Remind him to Sit as you leave and go to the other side, a few feet away. Turn to face him and command Hup.

Praise Champ **as** he jumps, not before. *Reward* him by letting him jump into the hose, but only **after** he has landed properly.

Next time, leave Champ just **slightly** to the other side of the center of the jump. Repeat the same exercise.

Gradually increase the distance from the center over many training sessions until Champ jumps the hurdle even when left facing the upright jump standard.

Do not leave Champ further off center than the edge of the jump. You **always** stand in the center. Remember, we are trying to make him successful, not create a problem.

If your dog tries to come around the jump at any time, **calmly** tell him No as you move toward the side of the jump he is approaching. By moving out of position and not allowing him to come, you have interrupted the exercise so he knows something has gone wrong.

Gently take him back to the place you left him, but position him slightly closer to the center line. Return to the other side of the jump, but tap the top as you tell him Hup.

Anytime your dog tries to go around the jump, back up to the last place he was successful. End that training session there with one correct jump.

If your dog tries to go around the jump more than once, he needs much more **Foundation** work. Go back to jumping in a straight line until he is secure and consistent.

When you return to angle jumping, place obstacles such as chairs (or even two people) at the sides of the jump to discourage the bad habit already created. If you use people, their only function is to **prevent** your dog from coming around the jump, **not** to discipline him in any way.

SV trials require a brush jump. If you do not have one, simply drape a piece of green Astroturf over your jump to make it look similar. Then it won't be such a big surprise to your dog on trial day.

Four jumping efforts is the maximum for any training session. We are often tempted to do more because it is fun and Champ enjoys jumping. Drilling only creates boredom. Too many repetitions make him like it less.

And jumping a tired dog can cause injury. It also develops bad habits and a poor attitude. Quit while you are ahead – while Champ still wants to jump more.

Adding the Retrieve

Put retrieving and jumping together only when **both** are absolutely perfect themselves. A polished retrieve on the flat, and correct jumping technique from any place at any distance, mean you are ready to join the two.

Both retrieving and jumping must be correct habits for Champ before they are combined. Also, off-leash heeling **must** be stabilized and Champ should be able to heel while he is carrying the dumbbell.

Set the jump back to the height of your dog's withers. Attach the leash on the dead ring of the fur saver.

Begin with Champ in the basic position facing the jump, a reasonable distance away. Throw the dumbbell so it lands approximately the **same** distance on the far side of the jump as you are standing away from the jump on this side.

Heel Champ up to the base of the jump and command Hup. Let the leash go **slack** to allow him to jump.

As he jumps, you go around the hurdle and tell him Fetch. Leave the leash slack, but go to the dumbbell with him. After he picks it up, heel him back to the base of the jump and command Hup.

Leave enough slack in the leash to allow Champ to jump. Then heel him away in a straight line from the jump, praising him as he carries the dumbbell away.

62. ADD RETRIEVE ONLY WHEN JUMPING IS PERFECT.

Here you can vary what you do depending on what Champ likes best. You can grab the dumbbell and play tug-of-war, or get a front sit first before you play tug-of-war, or get a front sit and out for food and then tug-of-war with the dumbbell.

Use whatever works here to *reward* Champ for a complete exercise done correctly. Do this in the **exact** place where Champ will return with the dumbbell to associate this place with pleasure and fun (remember *place association*).

Two or three repetitions are quite enough for this complicated exercise. Quit as soon as Champ **begins** to show understanding, or when he improves even slightly.

This exercise shows Champ the entire retrieve over the hurdle while you control every move, preventing mistakes. When he consistently performs this exercise with precision and confidence, you are ready to take off the leash.

With Champ off-leash, lower the jump to withers height again. Have him in the basic position facing the jump, a comfortable distance for his **one** stride approach to take-off.

Toss the dumbbell to about the same distance on the other side. You always strive to make the distance between the dumbbell and the jump the **same** as the distance between yourself and the jump – ideally one stride for Champ.

Command Hup. While he is in the air over the jump, command Fetch.

If your dog has any hesitation in jumping back to you, help him with another Hup command. However, if you have done the on-leash exercise enough, he should understand this by now.

63. STAND IN FRONT OF WALL
TO PREVENT DOG FROM JUMPING OFF.

64. HEADING DOWN THE OTHER SIDE WITH DUMBBELL.

Again here, vary what you do when Champ brings you the dumbbell depending on what he enjoys most. One front sit every few sessions is quite enough. And **one** correct performance of this exercise is enough for any session.

When you incorporate retrieving into your routine from now on, the sequence is one flat retrieve and one over the jump, if you choose to jump him that session. (See Chapter 18: Putting It All Together.) **Always** do the retrieve on the flat ground well away from the hurdle, or with your back to the jump, to prevent any confusion.

<u>Scaling Wall</u>

We recommend waiting until Champ has earned his SchH. I title before teaching the scaling wall. Once the habit of soaring over the hurdle is stabilized, he usually avoids stepping on the jump.

Teaching the scaling wall too early, however, might create confusion. Now your dog learns that Hup can mean to **use** the jump to get over.

The scaling wall is taught exactly the same as the hurdle, except it needs even less *motivation* and distance away from the base. No speed is necessary here.

Proper training promotes the correct technique of rear end action. Teach Champ to use his engine (rear end) for power, not speed.

Champ needs to learn to thrust straight **up** the wall (Fig. 60, Page 214) and to climb **down** the other side (Fig. 63). Speed is counter-productive here because it makes your dog travel horizontally instead of vertically.

Caution: Be sure **any** scaling wall you use is sturdy and well-supported. Your dog is not comfortable climbing over an unsteady wall.

Spread the wall out slightly (Fig. 63), so it is a little lower than its full height for SchH. II. Heel Champ in a straight line toward the wall (just as in the hurdle progressions). When you are near the base, tap the center of the wall and command Hup.

As he climbs one side, you position yourself right at the bottom of the other side (Fig. 63), so he cannot jump off the top. Back up slowly so he climbs down carefully and then heel him away in a straight line.

For *motivation,* you can use the hose in front of your dog to encourage him to **climb** up the wall. Use it the same way on the other side to control his speed to make him **walk** down and not jump off. He then gets the hose at the base of the jump.

Follow the same progressions as in training Champ to jump over the hurdle. When leaving him on the other side of the wall, though, go to the **side** of the jump where you can see him. Then tap the middle of the jump. Be sure he is committed to jumping it **before** you go to the other side.

When you finally add the retrieve, throw the dumbbell close to the base of the scaling wall so he is not tempted to jump off the top when he sees it. Preferably, have another person on the other side of the wall to place the dumbbell properly after you throw it.

Remember that any time your dog does not jump, you are proceeding too quickly, if he is physically sound. Return to a step where he was successful and cement his **Foundation.**

Proofing

Proofing is done **only** when Champ jumps reliably and properly. Be sure he understands exactly what you want before adding any distractions.

Test this by walking in the area of the jump with Champ free on the field. As he gets near the jump, command Hup without any body language or hand signals.

If he looks for something to jump and then soars over it in proper form, praise him lavishly. If he looks confused, you have more training to do before adding distractions.

65. EXCELLENT HEIGHT AND ARC JUMPING OVER ONE METER HURDLE.

You can proof Champ over the jumps simply by having people standing nearby while he jumps. None of the people should be in his path for jumping, however.

Add distractions **only** for jumping. Proofing for retrieving is much more complex and should be done only for the retrieve, without any jumping.

<u>Patchwork</u>

Poor jumping technique, refusal, using the jump, or a dog consistently coming around the jumps can all result from lack of proper training. Be sure the dog is physically sound before beginning jumping work.

Unfortunately here, there really is no such thing as patchwork. There is only retraining.

Start at the beginning. Change his command to Over if your dog has a poor attitude or lacks confidence.

Consistent success usually leads to a reliable jumper. Step by step progressions ensure learning.

Be sure to spend even **more** time on each step with this dog. Remember that retraining always takes more time than starting from scratch.

<u>Puppy Imprinting</u>

Puppies are too awkward and clumsy to learn to jump correctly. The only *imprint* to make is that jumping is fun.

You can walk your puppy (at least four months old) up to a six-inch board and have him pop over as you say Hup.

If he hesitates, get in front and tap the jump for him to come to you. Make a big fuss of him when he jumps.

For a young dog, "huppers" can be great fun. When you are walking a young dog and see a small obstacle (such as a bench or low log) run up to it with him. Jump over it with him as you tell him Hup. Be sure the obstacles are **low** and the footing is good so he can't get into trouble.

When you do this often enough, your young dog learns to look for things to jump when you command Hup. He learns the word association and enjoys jumping.

Just be sure not to overdo this introduction. Keep it fun and not work.

Teaching jumping technique not only makes your dog correct, it is also safer and prevents injury in the long run. Taking time for the proper **Foundation** lasts a lifetime.

66. A FUTURE PERFECT JUMPER.

67. THE START OF A FLYING VORAUS.

Chapter 15

The Flying Voraus

A dog is the only thing on earth
that loves you more than he loves himself.
— Josh Billings

Goal: For the dog to heel correctly, fly away from the handler at top speed when released, and continue running straight until downing instantly on command.

The voraus is one of the most challenging exercises because it represents that delicate, elusive balance between *motivation* and control. It also is the ultimate test of training and *stamina* because it comes at the **end** of the routine, when the dog may be tired and possibly stressed too.

Place association is the easiest and most reliable way to teach the voraus. Champ learns that he **always** runs down the center line, in the direction of the recall, to just past the spot where you stood for his recall.

Thus you begin training the voraus when Champ is familiar with the long, straight heeling down the center line and comes in fast on the recall. Add the down when he has a functional down. By this time he has a clear perspective of directions and locations on the training field – what happens where and when.

VORAUS EXERCISE

From starting place on center line of field:
- Begin in basic position (sit). Acknowledge judge.
- Normal heeling for a few paces.
- Simultaneously raise arm, command Voraus and stop.
- Lower arm, or keep it raised until after dog lies down.
- When dog reaches desired distance, command Down.
  (Judge may tell you when to command Down.)
- Upon signal from judge, proceed to dog's right side.
- Command Sit.
- Exercise is complete when dog returns to basic position.

SchH. I voraus is at least 25 paces.
SchH. II voraus is at least 30 paces.
SchH. III voraus is at least 40 paces.

Foundation: Teaches the dog to run out quickly in a straight line and lie down when told.

Begin training the voraus on a cool day when Champ is full of energy. After a very **short** heeling pattern, one sit in motion and recall from down, play hoses as usual after the recall.

Choose a place on your training field which will **always** be the target for voraus **Foundation** work, just past where you stand to recall Champ. Always use a **visible** target here.

If you have a goalpost or tree in the right place, hang up your bait pouch (or the hose) where Champ can clearly see it, but cannot reach it even if he jumps up. If you do not have anywhere to hang his target, use a small bucket.

232

From a few inches away, focus Champ on the target with your right hand as you place food (or hose) there (Fig. 68). Hold him by the fur saver collar with your left hand. Hold him back firmly (to incite his *opposition reflex*) as you excite him and help him focus on the target (Fig. 69).

When he is looking at the target intently and straining to get to it (Fig. 69), turn back down the field and take him several feet away. Always lead him by the collar or tab. Do not ask him to heel. Turn back to face the target.

Psyche Champ up again until he focuses on the target (Fig. 70) and pulls to go to it (Fig.71). Place your open **right** hand beside his head to give him the direction you want him to go (Figs. 70 & 71).

Use your voice to energize and excite him. Say the same words each time to psyche him up, such as Ready? Want To Go Get It?

When Champ looks **directly** at the target, let him go with the command Voraus (Fig. 72). Walk after him.

When he gets there, allow him to eat the food (Fig. 73), or grab the hose, on the bucket. If your target is up high, take it down and feed him (or play tug-of-war with the hose) and praise him. You are always right behind him to *reward* him when he reaches the target.

Play two hoses energetically in that spot, but only for a few short tosses if you are not finished training this session. Save Champ's energy for the voraus today.

Repeat the same exercise again. Show him the baited target, and then take him several feet away, just where you did before, and psyche him for the target.

If Champ ran straight out to the target the last time,

68. SHOW DOG BAITED TARGET.

69. PSYCHE DOG UP FOR TARGET.

70. TAKE DOG BACK SEVERAL FEET
AND REFOCUS HIM USING YOUR RIGHT ARM.

71. PSYCHE DOG UP AND
INCITE OPPOSITION REFLEX TO GO.

72. LET GO WHEN DOG IS FOCUSED.

73. LET HIM RUN TO TARGET AND EAT FOOD.

take him back a few more feet this time. Add more distance **only** if the last one was straight and correct.

Psyche Champ up and send him again **as soon as** he looks directly at the target. Be sure you walked in a **straight** line and led him by the collar or tab, not heeling him. This allows him to concentrate on how to get back to the target.

Be sure to leave the target in **exactly** the same place every time, preferably just past where you stood for the recall. Then Champ can remember the spot (*place association*).

Also be sure to face Champ **toward** your voraus target and focus him right in front of it before leaving. Then take him by the collar to turn him around to go back down the field toward your starting point before sending him.

It is easy for Champ to learn that he always runs down the field in the **same** direction to the **same** place. That place is always just past where you stood on the recall.

Handling Notes

Depending on how Champ does on any day, two or three repetitions are plenty. Extend the distance, stopping and turning to psyche him up once or twice, until he is running **further** than a full-length voraus.

The voraus is like the recall – the longer it gets, the more motivational it becomes, and the faster Champ runs. Begin working at **more** than full distance as soon as possible.

This dovetails with making your recall longer than normal also. Both teach Champ to accelerate to full speed and keep going.

Be very aware of your dog's physical *condition* and

stamina when working on voraus. A tired dog soon gets slow and sour. We want Champ to learn the voraus only at full power. Avoid working on voraus when it is too hot.

Always end on a good note, with Champ running straight out to the target, eating and then playing. Shorten the distance if you need to, so Champ can end with success.

If your second voraus is good, end there. Avoid the "One-More-Time Syndrome," especially when working on voraus.

Always **walk** behind Champ whenever you release him for voraus. You need to be there to *reward* him, but **running** after him can worry him, distract him or break his focus on where he is going.

If your dog has any trouble finding the target, or if he constantly wants to use his nose to find it, make it more visible. If you have nowhere to hang your bait pouch, be sure to put enough food on the bucket to keep Champ busy until you get there to give more food, praise and then play.

Adding the Down

Once Champ is highly motivated, focuses well and runs directly out to the target, begin adding the down. He should already have a functional down before using it here. Return to a **shorter** distance for the voraus.

Use the same routine as before to create Champ's desire to run out quickly and directly. Walk after him so you are right behind him when he reaches the target. If you are using a bucket, put only a little food on it this time.

Just as he gets there, command Down. He probably won't go down immediately. Giving him several commands for down here is normal.

Keep your tone of voice pleasant but firm. Remember that he doesn't know this exercise yet. He eventually downs quickly when he learns where his *reward* always comes.

Because this voraus is shorter than usual, you arrive on the scene quickly. Tell Champ Down and, when he does, continue to feed him between his legs, **while** he is in down position. Remind him Down as you give him the hose **while** he is down.

Then release and play two hoses. Always play **past** the voraus target so the *reward* stays in the right place.

As you lengthen the distance for the voraus, use a securely closed container with food inside under the target bucket (if you have nowhere to elevate your pouch). Put only one or two pieces of food on the target now.

When Champ arrives at the target, command Down. Praise him when he lies down. When you arrive, continue to tell him Down, Good Dog, as you open the container. Feed him in down position while you praise. Release and play.

If your target is raised, praise him for lying down while you get the target. Feed him in down position while you continue to praise. Release and play.

Once he learns to down here, keep him down for at least 10 to 20 seconds **every** time with continual feeding between his legs. This prepares him to stay down while you eventually walk all the way up the field.

About the time the voraus is consistent and Champ is

downing fairly well, you begin working on different fields. Find one with a place to elevate the target and use that method to stabilize the down.

Always praise when Champ lies down, then feed and play after the down at the end of his voraus. This *motivation* and *reward* is what Champ remembers.

This is also an excellent place to practice the down while playing two hoses. (See **Polishing** in Chapter 9: Dynamic Down.) Use this technique sparingly, however. Remember that two hoses is Champ's game, not a time for nagging obedience. Remember to keep the play **past** the place you want Champ to down on the voraus, not in front of it.

Stabilizing the voraus takes many repetitions. Continue working at this progression until you can **heel** Champ all the way back to your starting point, quickly psyche him up, and he flies all the way down the field to the target and downs with one or two commands.

Each time, use the unreachable hose or food, whichever works best to motivate your dog. Then **always** *reward* him with what he wants.

If the down is still sticky, work on it more during play time off the field. Pretend to throw the hose and, as your dog runs **away** from you, command Down.

When he turns and downs, praise him lavishly. Go to him and remind him Down as you place the hose in front of his mouth. Let him grab it while he is down, then quickly release and play. If he is a real chow hound, go to him and toss food between his front legs sometimes before giving him the hose.

When Champ is going down quickly and solidly during play, you can progress to **throwing** the hose to him as you release him to catch it. Remember to use this technique sparingly though. This type of trickery (only **pretending** to throw the hose and commanding Down) is the best way to break down your dog's trust.

Any time your dog does not down when you command him, avoid giving him a second command. Take him back calmly (firmly but gently) to the **exact** place where you wanted him to down. Have him down and then praise, pet, feed and play.

Continue to do the voraus **immediately** after the recall for many training sessions. When going to new fields, practice **only** the recall and then the voraus.

Doing just these two exercises together, as a pair, especially on a new field, helps Champ learn that the voraus goes to the recall spot. After each recall, turn and show Champ the target (holding him by the collar) before taking him back down the field for the voraus.

Interrupt these two exercises with a retrieve **only** when both the retrieve and voraus are completely trained and polished.

When training this type of motivational voraus, always remember to throw your dumbbell **away** from the direction of the voraus target when you add the retrieves. We don't want Champ sailing past the dumbbell to get the voraus target you just showed him, or remembering where the dumbbell landed on his way down the field for voraus.

Once Champ is flying down the field and going down reliably, it is time to begin weaning him away from a visible target. After the recall, turn and hold Champ by the collar and throw the hose just past the recall spot so he sees it.

Return to your starting position, focus Champ and excite him about going, and send him on the voraus. When he gets to where the hose is, command Down.

You walk quickly behind Champ. When he downs, praise him with Good Dog, Down.

When you get to where he is down, toss a few pieces of food between his front legs and praise him. While he is busy eating the food, pick up the hose.

Give him the hose **while** he is down. Then release and play. Play two hoses for several minutes to *reward* a job well done.

Once Champ is doing a full-length voraus reliably for just the tossed hose, you can begin to test occasionally. Instead of throwing the hose after the recall, turn and only **pretend** to throw it.

Follow your usual procedure, but just as Champ gets to where the hose **should** be, command Down. Be sure to command Down **before** he drops his nose to find it. If he slows down or tries to sniff it out before he goes far enough, more **Foundation** work is needed and more practice on down.

Walk after Champ as soon as he leaves your side. When he downs, praise him. He doesn't get up if you have separated praise and release properly during training.

As you reach him, toss a few pieces of food between his front legs. Walk **past** him and pretend to pick up the hose. Be sure he sees it so he thinks it was there all the time.

Call him to you and play. Or return to his side, praise, pet him, feed and then give him the hose while he is down. Release and play **past** the place where he downed.

Occasionally you can use the hose (and/or food) to have Champ come to the sit at your side from the down. But teach this first with the long down. (See Up to Sit in Chapter 16: Long Distance Down.)

Test the voraus without the hose only rarely. We want Champ to **believe** his hose is always out there, not to discover we're trying to trick him.

When Champ has done an exceptionally fast voraus and gone down immediately, as you are walking out to him, **toss** the hose you have to him. Then play two hoses **past** the place where he downed.

Use this only rarely, however. We don't want the dog to turn early because he knows we have another hose. But we do want him to learn that we always *reward* his instant response to Down.

Reward him in this way **only** if he was very quick to down and there was absolutely no anticipation. This is a special treat for when Champ does an excellent job.

Polishing: Creates correct heeling in the build-up, channeling energy for the voraus.

Polishing for the voraus is much like the polishing done for the retrieve. Channeling the *drive* into heeling creates an even more explosive voraus.

Until now, you have been holding Champ's collar before sending him. Now start making him sit before allowing him to go.

When he sits, feed him in position. Rewarding this sit

makes this part of the exercise easier. Fighting with him to wait only creates forging because of *opposition reflex* and the high *motivation* built for the voraus.

Feed him until he is calmly sitting in correct position beside you. Then take hold of his collar briefly, focus him on the target, and send him. When he is doing this correctly, begin sending him from a sit.

Once Champ is sitting solidly before being sent, and still doing a straight voraus from the sit, add five or six steps of heeling. Hold him by the collar and psyche him up first. Then have him sit. Then heel a few paces.

Insist on **correct** heeling. Feed almost continually to prevent any forging and remind him Heel.

Halt after a few steps and make him sit again. *Reward* this sit with food also.

If Champ has lost focus at all, hold him by the collar again and psyche him up again until he looks down the field at the target. Have him sit again, feed him, and then send him.

Send him from a sit consistently from now on. Vary the number of heeling paces before the second sit.

Send Champ from heeling only rarely. This is only a test! Regularly sending him from a sit prevents anticipation in the build-up heeling.

Once Champ is steady and secure in his control work before being sent on the voraus, you can polish it even further by insisting on an Attention Sit. Now you feed him when he looks at you and allow him to go **only** from the Attention Sit. (See **Polishing** in Chapter 7: The Solid Sit.)

Patchwork

A slow or crooked voraus can be difficult to fix. However, if you begin *place association* to the recall spot with a clearly **visible** target, most dogs catch on after many repetitions.

For a slow voraus, try using a sleeve as the target. Give the dog a bite **only** after he downs correctly.

Reteaching the basics included in voraus (fast recall, motivational down, correct heeling, Attention Sit) often go a long way in improving this exercise.

Puppy Imprinting

Teaching a young dog to run out a few feet to a clearly **visible** target (such as a bucket), on which there is a pile of food (Figs. 68 to 73), can be very motivational. While he eats the food, quietly but quickly walk out to him and praise and play two hoses for a brief time when you get there.

Such an introduction makes a correct *imprint*. But, as with all puppy activity, it must not be overdone. Take him only a few feet from the target.

A short voraus is all a very young dog can master. Lack of coordination and concentration limit the immature dog much more than we realize – often until it is too late and we have pushed them one step too far.

A flying voraus with an immediate down makes a great final impression on the judge. It also proves you know how to strike the correct balance in your training between *motivation* and control.

Chapter 16

Long Distance Down

There's facts about dogs, and there's opinions about them.
The dogs have the facts, and the humans have the opinions.
— J. Allen Boone

Goal: To have the dog remain down quietly and calmly, in the same place, regardless of where the handler is.

The long down is by far the most neglected exercise in Schutzhund obedience. It is also a most frustrating way to lose major points.

What seems on the surface to be the most simple exercise in the routine, can be very difficult for the dog. The long down puts the dog in the greatest conflict with his natural survival instincts.

The dog is a social animal. That is why wolves live in packs. It is totally contrary to their nature to remain alone. A wolf alone in the wild must struggle to survive.

The social dog is now required to assume a submissive position and remain there **alone**. Add to this the temptation of being able to see his handler (whom he considers a pack member, ideally his leader) in SchH. I and II. He can also see another dog (a stranger to him and thus possibly an intruder),

245

LONG DOWN EXERCISE

At the side of the field, near appropriate flag (male or female):
- Begin in the basic position (sit). Acknowledge judge.
- Remove leash and put away or secure it (SchH. I and II).
- Command Down.
- Once dog is down, walk straight away, about 40 paces.
- Upon the judge's signal, return to right side of dog.
- Command Sit.
- Attach leash (SchH. I and II).
- Exercise is complete when dog is in basic position.

For SchH. III the handler goes out of sight of the dog.

---

running, jumping and chasing clearly within his view. All his instincts tell him to join his pack and check out this intruder.

So don't take this exercise for granted. Take the time to build a solid, secure long down.

Foundation: Teaches the dog to remain in one place and rewards him for doing so.

Begin your training for the long down when Champ has a functional down. Always start in a quiet place free from noise and distractions.

The long down is an exercise in **concentration** for your dog, not sleeping or being distracted. A dog dozing or watching what is going on too intently can forget what he is supposed to be doing.

The side of your regular training field is a fine place to start. Avoid doing the long down while another dog works until Champ's **Foundation** is complete. Distractions and temptations come later.

Heel Champ to your chosen location at the **side** of the field. Use *place association* and put Champ down in exactly the **same** spot for the first few weeks of this training.

Halt and *reward* a correct sit with food. Reach down and **pretend** to take off the leash, but leave it on.

Champ **never** does any moving exercises with his leash on. (This can be dangerous and inhibiting.) For now the leash serves as an extra signal that no action is imminent.

Command Down in your normal tone of voice. Drop three or four pieces of food between his front legs.

Look for a visual marker so you can tell **exactly** where you left Champ when you return. If there is no such indicator on the ground, feed Champ a few more pieces of food and, while he is eating, place the leash even with his front paws, but in front of **your** feet.

Feed a few more pieces of food and remind him Down just before you walk about three feet away. Remember that you never do recalls or front sits from this medium distance.

Stand **sideways** to Champ. Turning to face him could cue a recall. Standing with your back to him means you are unable to watch him.

The key to creating a relaxed, confident, correct long down is random *positive reinforcement*. While Champ is lying still, and at least about every 10 to 30 seconds at first, return to Champ and feed him between his front legs.

As you reach Champ, stand in front of him. Calmly tell him Down, Good Dog and toss him a couple more pieces of food between his front legs. Remind him Down as you leave again.

Return and feed Champ from the **front.** Going all the way back to heel position signifies the end of the exercise. Walking around him just encourages him to turn to watch you and could make him move.

Return to Champ frequently and reinforce his **good** behavior. Waiting until he moves, and then returning to correct him, only makes your dog nervous and unsure.

Should your dog move or inch forward, you can tell because you noted a visual marker on the ground, or used the leash to indicate where you left him. **Always** return him (without corrections yet) to the **exact** place where you left him and then feed there.

Time and Distance

Vary the time between returning and feeding, from 10 to 30 seconds at first. Extend the time for the long down by 30 seconds per training session until Champ waits calmly for at least five minutes. Now begin increasing the distance you leave by about three feet each session.

While extending the distance, reduce the time again. Go back to returning and feeding between 10 to 30 seconds when you go further away.

You can increase either the time (by 30 second intervals), or the distance (by three feet each time), but not both together. Increase either time or distance each time Champ is successful at the present level.

If your dog ever begins to fidget or whine, or just looks

uneasy, return to the previous level where he was secure and sure. **One** long down at each training session is sufficient.

Once Champ is calmly remaining in place for up to five minutes while you are 20 feet away, increase the distance each time by three feet until he is staying down for **one** minute while you are 30 feet away. Then go back to only 10 feet away and increase the time by **one** minute intervals until he is staying for up to 10 minutes with only a few food rewards.

Only when Champ is secure with both time and distance separately do you add them together. Once he has stayed down the full time with you 30 feet away, repeat this only once or twice in several training sessions.

At most sessions, do the long down for only a short time, or at a close distance, returning to feed. Continual long downs become boring for your dog and only invite trouble.

Up to Sit

Vary whether you practice the long down before or after the working routine. When you return to Champ to pick him up, go directly to heel position **beside** him, not **around** him.

Feed him a few more pieces of food, reminding him Down, to prevent anticipation. The first few times, you must teach him **how** to get to a sit from the down.

Reach down and show him a piece of food in your left hand in front of his nose. Command Sit, in a pleasant tone. Raise the food up so that he follows it until he is **all the way** up in a sit.

249

Feed him and praise him calmly. Stabilize this sit by feeding him a few more pieces in correct position.

Heel Champ away for a few steps and then interrupt heeling with an energetic release and allow him to bite the hose. Release and *reward* only **correct** heeling.

This prepares Champ for a trial, when you want him to spring back into *drive* for the working phase if he has done the long down first. Vary the direction you heel him away, either forward or to the back, since this varies in trials.

Energize Champ with playing two hoses here for a few minutes. We want him to **expect** something fun is going to happen after you pick him up from the long down.

Proofing

When Champ's **Foundation** for the long down is complete, begin working with distractions. Start proofing with Champ down in the same location as usual.

While introducing distractions, attach Champ's six-foot leash to his fur saver collar. You go only to the end of the leash at first to prevent any mistakes.

The first distraction is another dog heeling on the center line of the field. No playing yet.

Return to Champ often and toss food between his front feet, especially when he shows interest in what the other dog is doing. Remind him Down, Good Dog, as you do.

Next add gunfire during the long down, once you know Champ is gunsure in other circumstances. Use a gun that is not too loud at first and keep it far away.

Again you are at the end of a six-foot leash, as you are for all distraction training. Each time the gun goes off, return to Champ and feed him, repeating Down, Good Dog.

Next progress to another dog performing the complete routine, including recall and retrieves. Return to feed Champ immediately after the recall command and retrieves.

If Champ is solid throughout all of this, add the distraction of a dog playing up and down the center line. Keep this excitement moderate at first.

Progress to another dog playing closer to Champ **only** when he has been consistently steady and solid during all other distractions. The final proofing in this place is to have another person approach Champ and walk near him.

When Champ is solid through all the distractions, you are ready to go to new places. Shorten both distance and time when working in a new location.

If at any time your dog fails to remain down, simply prevent his escape with the six-foot leash. Calmly take him back to the **exact** place where he was down. Command Down, feed him, praise him (no petting), and go back to the end of the leash.

When you take your dog back after he has broken, put him down without having him sit beside you again. Beginning from heel position tells him you are starting over again and nothing really went wrong.

Bringing him **directly** back to the spot by the collar and making him down immediately tells him something went wrong. No gruff voice or harsh corrections, however. He needs to learn what is right, as well as what is wrong.

There is no need for anger or other negative emotions here. You are **teaching** Champ, not testing yet.

Proofing is to show your dog how to handle distractions and make his own decisions. It should make him confident and successful, not nervous and worried.

Introducing Corrections

Once proofing is complete, Champ is solid and clear on what is expected during the long down. If he has had trouble settling in with any specific area (time, distance or distractions), continue working on those issues before adding any type of correction.

Now Champ does a short down at least one out of every three training sessions. By now he stays down off leash, while another dog works, with you at almost full distance, returning and feeding only a few times during each long down.

Begin turning your back to Champ, but **only** when you have someone else nearby who can watch him for you. Introduce going out of sight for a short time (less than one minute), also while someone else watches him for you. Put a blind on the field for this.

Should your dog break the long down, say nothing. Calmly and quietly walk to where he is, take him gently by the collar over to where you left him down.

Here you use his prong collar to make a strong downward correction as you calmly command Down. The correction is with his collar, not your voice. Feed, praise, remind Down and leave again.

If your dog ever breaks any down, he wears a six-inch tab attached to both rings of his prong collar for **every** subsequent training session. This maximizes your ability to correct him properly.

Any correction comes in the **exact** place he was disobedient, not wherever you happen to catch him. After every correction comes food and praise. He must know when he is right, as well as when he is wrong. Then there must be something in it for him to be right!

A dog who breaks more than once or twice is telling you to back up. This dog's **Foundation** is not secure.

Polishing: Teaches the dog to concentrate on holding still.

Polishing is not really necessary for the long down. But you can make Champ more solid in the down, even when tempted. And you can make his sit more flashy.

Polish only after proofing is finished and Champ is solid in all circumstances. Prepare Champ for the long down by starting from the basic position as usual.

Command Down. When he does, show him the hose. Be sure he remains solidly down. Feed him between his front legs to *reward* his correct behavior.

Praise and continue feeding, reminding him Down, as you walk around in front of him. When he shows you he is really solid, even when tempted by seeing the hose, progress to teaching him to sit up quickly.

Still showing him the hose, return to his side. Command Sit. Remind him Sit as you slowly lower the hose to just in front of his mouth.

Let him bite the hose in position. Release him and play tug-of-war. Then have him release the hose and heel a few steps, insisting on correct position. Use the hose to *reward* him during heeling. Play tug-of-war and then play two hoses. This energizes him from the down and prepares him for working.

Whenever you use the hose to create a faster sit, **always** feed Champ several times between his front legs while he is still down. We don't want him to break the down while we teach him to sit up quickly on command.

Use this *motivation* for the sit only occasionally, once the sit is fast and complete for food. Be careful to *reward* **only** a complete sit, all the way up beside you.

Polishing, in the sense we use it, means making the dog more intense within the exercise. The long down is one place we want Champ relaxed. He only needs to bounce back into *drive* for the pick-up sit.

Patchwork

There is no quick fix for the long down exercise. Problems arise because of lack of **Foundation**, which means this dog really doesn't know what to do or how to concentrate.

Many dogs are uncomfortable on the long down because it has never been a pleasant place to be. The only time the handler returned was to correct him.

For a dog who is nervous, or shows avoidance when the handler comes close, simply return often and toss food between his front legs. It takes some time to convince this dog you're not going to correct him every time you return, so be patient and persevere.

These dogs are often reliable on the long down, but they look depressed or nervous. They present a poor picture.

As you develop a more trusting relationship with this dog through motivational obedience, the long down becomes more relaxed and stable also. You're on your way to putting a better **Attitude** back in your team.

Puppy Imprinting

The long down *imprint* is made with a young dog simply by feeding him constantly while he's lying down. Keep him busy by tossing food, piece by piece, between his front legs. (See Fig. 36, Page 151.)

Even a young dog can learn to accept and enjoy lying down when it means there is something in it for him. Keep it short, however.

Even with constant feeding, several seconds is the absolute longest you can **rely** on a puppy to hold his concentration, even on food. Quit while you are ahead and clearly release him before he makes a mistake.

The next time you watch a Schutzhund trial, watch the dogs on the long down. Their composure tells you not only about their temperament, but about their training.

Take your time in building a solid down. Your reward is not having to worry about this exercise in the future.

74. STEADYING THE STAND.

Chapter 17

Steady Stands

A dog likes to obey.

It gives them security.
– James Herriot

Goal: To produce a steady, solid, secure stand immediately on command.

Teach the stand **after** Champ has his SchH. II title. Wait until he is doing the sit and down quickly, consistently and with confidence. You can teach the stand position earlier, but keep this work away from the training field until you are ready to train for SchH. III.

It takes enough time and effort to achieve a functional **Foundation** and then polish the first two moving exercises successfully. Keep these two exercises clear for Champ.

Teaching the stand too early can cause a period of confusion. Be **certain** your dog is sure of the sit and down commands before adding the stand.

The "famous SchH. III sit" (where the dog stands solidly for the moving sit) is usually caused by not stabilizing the sit in motion properly, or a change in the handler's command.

STAND EXERCISES

From starting place on center line after recall from down:
- Begin in basic position (sit). Acknowledge judge.
- At least 10 paces normal heeling.
- Command Stand as you continue walking.
- Proceed 30 paces. Turn to face dog.
- On judge's signal, return to right side of dog.
- After a few seconds, command Sit.
- Exercise is complete when dog assumes basic position.
- If you praise or pet dog here, assume new basic position.
- From that basic position, acknowledge judge.
- At fast pace, heel at least 10 paces.
- Command Stand as you continue running.
- Continue running at least 30 paces. Turn to face dog.
- On judge's signal, call dog.
- After dog sits in front for a few seconds, finish dog.
- Exercise is complete when dog assumes basic position.

Tone of voice is especially critical to your dog's success in the motion exercises. The phonetic sounds of "sit" and "stand" are extremely similar.

Dogs have exceptional hearing, but they do not naturally use this gift to differentiate between words. Your **tone** of voice is a more effective signal to Champ.

Use a clear upward inflection for Sit. Command Down in a stronger, deeper tone of voice. Make Stand soft, and much smoother than the other two words.

Champ also learns faster when you keep the moving exercises in sequence. Then he knows there is **always** one sit, one down and two stands.

Stand Position

Teach the stand position initially off the field, or even at home first. By now you and Champ are completely comfortable with food steering.

Begin with Champ simply walking or standing nearby. Go to his side with food in your closed hand.

Place your hand just in front of his nose, but lower than you use for the sit. Keep the food just **below** his muzzle. While he stands, repeat Stand as you allow him to eat the food.

If your dog tries to sit or down because of previous training, close your hand (with food in it) and move it forward. Encourage your dog to stand again. Feed him **as soon as** he is standing and repeat the command.

Teach this in one place until he begins to understand and associate the word with this new position. Continue using constant *positive reinforcement* until Champ is sure and secure standing still.

Once he is on his way to learning this new command, repeat this sequence in different places throughout the day. When he responds well, without trying to move or sit, introduce this exercise on the training field.

Foundation: Teaches the dog to stand by stopping his forward motion and rewarding correct position. Makes the dog comfortable and secure standing still.

After doing a moving sit and recall from down, you now have a new starting place – at the opposite end, facing back down the field. Heel Champ at least 12 paces, feeding rhythmically.

As you command Stand in a calm, smooth tone of voice, stop by his side and feed Champ as you have been doing off the field. Continue feeding him in this position as you repeat Stand, Good Dog.

This exercise is one of the easiest to teach at this point. Champ already understands remaining in a specific position for food. All his previous training makes him attentive, willing and cooperative because he knows he gets what he wants by responding correctly.

Once he is fairly consistent and steady, begin to alternate between *positive reinforcement* and *reward*. Intermittently withhold the food for a few seconds after saying Stand, then feed.

Continue this training, sometimes guiding him into the stand and sometimes feeding him just after he stands on command. At this point, you **always** stop beside him.

Release **backwards** or to the side for this exercise. Thus your dog does not get the idea of moving forward. Be sure to release calmly here. This exercise requires calm concentration and control, not energy.

Begin heeling Champ again and repeating the above exercise. When teaching, repeat the exercise two or three times per session.

Stop when Champ shows progress. Put him away for his quiet time **immediately** after working on this new exercise.

Train the stand within the pattern each time. Champ already has a good idea of what comes next, in which direction. Going in the opposite direction helps him learn this new exercise.

Standing Alone

Once Champ is standing readily, even without being guided by food, and holding the position while you praise and feed, begin moving slightly **after** he is standing properly. First have him stand properly with you stopping beside him.

Remind him Stand and feed him. Then be sure you have no food in your hand. Walk forward only **one** step at first, then return to his side. Feed, praise calmly and then release clearly.

Always return **directly** to Champ's right side. Walking around only encourages him to turn his head to look at you. It invites him to break position or move his feet to watch as you walk behind him.

As Champ becomes more secure, standing solidly while you leave, increase the distance you leave to several steps in the direction you were heeling. Continue to halt beside him **first**, feed him there, and remind him Stand before you move away.

Always feed Champ on the build-up heeling to prevent anticipation, but be sure your hand is empty when you walk away and return. **After** you return, take out the food and feed while reminding him Stand. Then praise calmly and release clearly, backwards or sideways.

Standing Still

Continue this sequence, moving a few more steps forward (away from Champ) each time before you return. To be sure he stands in the same place, keep an eye on him or have someone else watch him while you walk away.

If you work mostly by yourself, take note of **exactly** where you left your dog so you can be sure he didn't move. If there is no natural marker, place a small stick or marker of some sort beside **your** right foot (in line with your dog's front feet). Feed him while you do this so he doesn't notice.

Placing anything in front of your dog's feet only encourages him to sniff and investigate it. When you return, if you notice he has moved (even slightly) past your marker, return to going only one or two steps past him until he is more solid in his stand.

As you are training this, begin weaning him from any hand movement as you command Stand. Remember that he responds to your hand motion to feed him, long before he knows the command.

Walking Stand

Once Champ is consistently standing confidently while you walk away, begin teaching him to stand while you keep moving. After **at least** 10 steps of heeling, command Stand and hesitate just slightly, until Champ stands still.

Take only one or two steps past him the first few times. Return to his side, feed, praise calmly and then release.

Continue this sequence, hesitating for less and less time, until Champ stands **immediately** upon your command, whether you continue moving or not. Then gradually add more distance.

Champ often begins to anticipate the stand during this process. Remember that anticipation is the beginning of learning.

He is only doing what you are teaching. Correction is unfair. Simply add more food during heeling to **prevent** any anticipation.

Also remember to use a quiet, smooth voice for the stand command. Keep your **tone** of voice distinct from your sit and down commands.

Continue these sequences until Champ stands readily without any hand signal or hesitation from you, and remains still no matter how far you walk past him. Continue to practice the sit in motion and the running down for SchH. III (in sequence) before working on the stand.

Should Champ stand for the moving sit, understand that this is also just anticipation. It is an effort to do what you are teaching. This is **not** a disobedience and does not need correction at this time.

Go back to pivoting directly in front of Champ when you command Sit (as you did in **Foundation** training). Then feed and praise when he sits. Higher *reward* clears up this confusion over time.

Avoid drilling these motion exercises. One sit in motion is enough. A second one may be done if your dog makes a mistake the first time. One down with recall is sufficient.

Two or three stands are enough for each session. If you want to do more training, practice off the field, with at least four hours of quiet time for Champ between sessions. Work **only** on the stand, with a limit of three to four repetitions per session.

Proofing

Begin proofing by adding distractions and temptations once Champ consistently holds a solid stand. First add one person standing several feet to his side.

Remain close to remind your dog Stand in case he loses his concentration. If any confusion arises during proofing, return to **Foundation** and stabilize the stand first.

Once Champ's stand is steady with another person nearby, they can begin walking within a few feet of him. They never walk behind him, however, as this only encourages him to look back and possibly move his feet.

Remember to return to Champ every few seconds throughout proofing. Praise, feed and remind him Stand before leaving again.

If you are alone, use petting as a distraction to steady his stand. After having Champ stand correctly, touch and stroke him to be sure he stays in position.

When he does, next time use your left hand to apply **slight** downward pressure on his shoulder blades (not his back) while reminding him Stand. Then assume your correct body position – praise, feed and calmly release.

Once Champ accepts this pressure and stands solidly, use it occasionally after you return to his side. When he resists the pressure (*opposition reflex* now works **for** you) and remains standing – praise, feed and release.

This helps prevent anticipation of sitting when you return to his side. Sitting too early, before the command, becomes more likely when Champ has shown in several SchH. III trials and knows what happens next.

Proofing techniques aim to stabilize an exercise and enhance understanding, not create new problems. Always give your dog a fair chance to learn, but discontinue distractions or procedures which do not suit his particular temperament.

Polishing: Sharpens the dog's response to the command. Makes him lock up immediately and stand solidly. Improves the sit.

Begin by creating a "suitcase" with your leash. Slip the leash under Champ's flank, just in front of his stifles, and pass the leash through its handle. Then attach the snap to the dead ring of the fur saver collar (Fig. 74, Page 256). A two or three-foot leash works best with most dogs.

Now heel Champ, feeding as usual. Continue heeling and feeding until Champ pays no attention to the loop around his flank.

Within the routine, after **at least** 12 paces heeling down the center line, quietly command Champ to Stand. Be sure to give the command **before** you use the leash!

Right after the command, use a surprise pop on the leash to bring Champ into the correct position immediately.

Use **upward** tension on the loop above his flank to prevent him from sitting down, and slight **backward** tension on the collar to stop his forward movement (Fig. 74).

Make the pop short and in the right direction. Avoid any long tension on the "suitcase" as this creates detrimental *opposition reflex*.

As Champ stands in correct position, proceed 5 to 10 paces forward. Then return and quietly praise and feed as you repeat Stand, Good Dog calmly several times.

Stand beside Champ and keep your feet still. Praise and feed. Reassure him he is in the correct position, while softly repeating the command. Stand is a calm exercise for you both.

Allow him to absorb what just happened and concentrate on his position. Once Champ has stood still for a few seconds, release backwards.

Continue using the "suitcase" stand most of the time now to prevent your dog from becoming too relaxed on this exercise. The dog should bring some positive body tension to this position, and **concentrate** on holding steady.

When Champ is consistently responding properly and shows a confident, steady stand, you can add temptation. This means introducing higher *motivation* as distraction.

Many dogs become too excited if you use the hose while first teaching the stand. Now Champ knows what to do, though, he learns to hold his position and **wait** to get what he wants.

Begin by doing the stand within the routine, feeding on the build-up. Return to his side and show him the hose as you remind him Stand.

Use food on the build-up heeling to prevent anticipation, but avoid having any food (or the hose) in your hand when you command Stand and use your "suitcase" leash. Always be sure to keep the food (or hose) **out of sight** as you return to Champ's side.

Slowly take the hose out as you keep reminding Champ to Stand. Lower the hose to just in front of his mouth.

Let him bite the hose **while** he is in position. Simultaneously release him and play tug-of-war.

You should notice Champ becomes more tense and rigid in his stand as he sees the hose. This positive body tension helps stabilize his position so he remains "frozen."

If at any time your dog moves out of position, use the "suitcase" to remind him of stand position. If he moves more than once, return to **Foundation** exercises. He is not ready for **Polishing** yet, or his *play drive* may be too high to be productive for this exercise.

When Champ can consistently hold the stand when he sees the hose, occasionally command Sit. Remind him Sit as you lower the hose to just in front of his mouth.

Let him bite it and simultaneously release and play tug-of-war. Use this *motivation* only occasionally, and only if Champ is super steady standing for food *reward*.

Practice the sit between the stand exercises very seldom. It only causes more anticipation and is not necessary. By now Champ **always** sits when told because he knows it is how to get what he wants from you.

The last step of **Polishing** is to insist on an Attention Sit (See Chapter 7: The Solid Sit) before release. Do this **only** when all other aspects of this exercise are absolutely solid.

<u>Running Stand</u>

When Champ is completely stable on the walking stand, prepare for the running stand. Begin by standing him as usual and stopping beside him.

Remind him Stand as you leave one or two steps and then **run** away for several more steps before returning. When Champ accepts this without moving, begin to run on the first or second step you take away from him.

Always stand Champ **first** and stop beside him. Remind him Stand and feed him, before leaving him at a slow run. Build up your speed and distance until Champ stands solidly no matter how fast you leave.

Once he accepts this, return and remind him to Stand. You back up one or two steps until you are standing beside his tail, still facing in the same direction he is.

Again remind him Stand, and then run **past** him, telling him Stand again, in the proper tone of voice, as you pass by him. Run only a few steps past at first before returning. Praise, feed and release backwards.

Do this at a slow run first, and run only a **few** steps past Champ. Return, feed, praise and release. Increase your speed and distance until you can run right past him, always reminding Stand in the correct **tone** of voice as you pass by him.

Once he remains standing steadily while you run by, introduce the running stand in sequence, after a successful walking stand. Run slowly the first few times and use your "suitcase" leash to teach him how to stand **immediately** on command, even from a run. This is a physical technique he needs practice to learn.

Testing

To be sure Champ understands the difference between the three commands, you can add the stand **occasionally** while playing hoses. As he comes close to you and drops one hose, command Stand as you take a giant step toward him to help stop his forward movement. Be **sure** to use the same quiet tone of voice he knows for that command.

If your dog does not lock up immediately, go to his side. Have him Stand. Remind him Stand as you lower the hose. Let him bite it as you release him. If your dog does not respond the second time you try this, stop doing this test.

Return to some **Foundation** and more **Polishing** exercises. Then be sure your proofing is finished. Try a free stand during hoses again many sessions later, when your dog understands the command more completely.

Always remember that hoses is Champ's game, not a time for nagging obedience. One out of every 10 times playing hoses is more than enough to use **any** command.

Continue to throw in one sit, one down and then a stand command (individually, not all in one session) about every 10 times you play hoses. This tests whether your dog really understands the difference between these three positions.

But this is **not** a time for any correction – verbal or physical. If he fails to respond properly, simply return to Show and Tell to get him in the right position.

This is a test! His response merely tells you how well he is learning what you are trying to teach. Respond by continuing training at the appropriate level.

When working in the routine, add the final basic sit **very** rarely. When you plan to practice that sit, use the proper **tone** of voice for that command. Apply downward pressure to Champ's shoulders while he is standing. If he is solid on the stand, then you can have him sit.

From the sit, release **calmly** if you do not go right into the running stand. This is not a place to play. Champ needs to be mentally prepared for the concentration needed for the running stand.

Adding the recall to the running stand needs to be done only rarely until Champ is a seasoned veteran. Returning, praising, feeding (or rewarding with the hose) and releasing helps create a more solid stand.

Introducing Corrections

Correcting a missed stand is usually useless. The moment is gone and correction after the fact (*punishment*) only causes confusion and stress.

Besides, this is almost always a **mistake**, not a **disobedience**. Thus correction is not needed.

When your dog misses a stand, back up a step and prevent the mistake the next time. (See following section.)

Be sure you have completed all the progressions, including proofing and **Polishing**. Give your dog time to learn the motion exercises in sequence before introducing any corrections.

If you find your dog is just becoming sloppy and not locking up, however, use a stronger "suitcase." For the next training session, attach the leash to both rings of his prong collar. Use the "suitcase" now as a correction, briskly and sharply in the proper direction, just as you give your Stand command calmly.

Be sure to **surprise** your dog with this correction. Avoid warning him with a different hand movement or a harsher command.

When done effectively, this correction takes your dog off his feet for a split second. This unsettling sensation usually spawns strict obedience to the command for some time.

If your dog continues to miss the stand, review Chapter 4: Corrections. Your technique was obviously not effective, or your dog does not have sufficient **Foundation** training.

Remember not to correct on the next few stands, but to give your dog a chance to learn. Allow him to recover from the stress of a correction.

Be sure your dog understands exactly what to do before giving a correction, and that your **tone** of voice is consistent. When he knows, and your correction is effective, it works the **first** time.

Preventing Mistakes

Remember that the dog's tendency is to sit when he stops moving because of all the **Foundation** training on the automatic sit. This creates an *imprint* that carries over during teaching the moving stand.

Once Champ knows the stand, try to prevent any mistakes by walking faster and using a softer tone of voice. When the dog sits, it is almost always a mistake and not a disobedience. Correction is not necessary and not productive.

Mistakes happen more in a trial because the dog is stressed or because the handler is nervous and changes his usual **tone** of voice. It is unlikely the dog knows the handler told him to sit, but decides to stand instead!

When mistakes happen in training, remain calm. Return to Show and Tell. Show Champ what you want and then Tell him he's a Good Dog. Praise sincerely, even though you **helped** him do it right.

Reward and release. Then do the exercise again using enough help to **prevent** your dog from making the same mistake the second time. End with success.

Patchwork

A dog who has been taught the stand through force is usually reliable, but often looks pressured. Be careful not to sacrifice correctness for enthusiasm.

After the dog stands on command – feed him, praise him and calmly stroke him in position. Reassure him every way you can that this is a comfortable place to be and that he is doing the right thing.

Try adding some of the **Polishing** techniques with the hose. Add *motivation* to make his task enjoyable.

Even if this dog never comes to enjoy the stand, accept that he is correct. He may never overcome his strong *imprint.*

Puppy Imprinting

Although you can teach a pup to stand for food, it is difficult for any young dog to stand still. And you can do nothing when he moves his feet. Because you do not need to teach the stand until after your dog is SchH. II, working on this position with the puppy is truly unnecessary and can lead to trouble.

Trying to get a young dog to concentrate on standing still, before he has the mental maturity and before he understands food steering, can make the wrong *imprint.* We want the stand to be a solid, steady exercise done with calmness. This is usually not possible with a puppy or with a young dog.

The stand can be a very touchy exercise. Take enough time to teach a strong **Foundation,** pay attention to the **tone** of your voice, and continue to practice the moving sit. Then Champ can learn this last exercise clearly and without confusion.

75. PUTTING IT ALL TOGETHER FOR SUCCESS.

Chapter 18

Putting It All Together

The bond with a true dog is as

lasting as the ties of this earth can be.
                                – Konrad Lorenz

So now you know the techniques for teaching Champ motivational obedience, exercise by exercise. But how do you put them all together?

Timetables differ for each dog. Some find certain exercises easier to learn and others more difficult.

How long your training takes before you are ready for trial depends on many variables – most critically your dog's drives and your ability as a trainer.

However, there are some general guidelines to prepare the big picture.

<u>Teaching Exercises</u>

Start with heeling on a quiet field. Remain on this familiar field, if possible, for most of Champ's **Foundation** training in all the exercises. Always teach new exercises on a quiet, familiar field.

Establish a starting point and use this **same** place every time. Continue up and down the center line until Champ's heel position is stable, attention is good and the right about turn is close and correct.

Add the right and left turns, and then the halt, when heel position is fairly stable. Always practice the same pattern, but keep each part a few strides **shorter** than required in the actual trial routine.

Once the automatic sit is consistently correct at the halt, begin teaching the sit in motion. Follow with the moving down. When the down is steady, begin to teach front sit from one step in front of Champ. Practice two or three front sits each time.

When the down is solid while you go the full length of the field, add the motivational recall. First do a few front sits from one step away.

Then have him down again (without build-up heeling) so Champ is facing the correct direction for the recall. *Reward* the down with food. Walk several steps away from Champ. Return to the front, praise and feed.

Drop several pieces of food between his front legs before you leave. End with a recall, going **further** away than in normal trial routine.

Interrupt recalls by throwing the hose (behind you) when Champ is still several feet away from you and coming full speed. End by playing the two-hose game for several minutes, standing near where you did the recall.

As Champ gets more fit, you can play two hoses for longer periods of time after the recall. Once he has more *stamina*, play hoses only a short time and then begin adding the voraus. Place your target after the recall.

After the voraus, play hoses again **past** the place you use for recall and voraus. Champ learns that this end of the field is **always** a fine place to be and streaks there for the recall and voraus!

Remember to practice all the exercises in the **same** order and direction they are performed in trial routine. We are not trying to trick Champ, but teach him what to expect.

After he is fully trained, then you can change the routine (except for the order of the motion exercises). This can keep Champ on his toes and make training more interesting.

But until Champ is a successful SchH. III competitor, the starting position is the same for heeling, moving sit and moving down. The recall and voraus are done to the same place in the same direction.

About the time you add voraus to your routine, introduce the heeling pattern for your group. As Champ's *stamina* and concentration increase, begin working on your group pattern between the two heeling patterns.

Once the front sit is stable, teach the finish from this position. Remember to start by stepping in front of Champ, not calling him into front sit. Even when both are functional, practice many more front sits **without** finishes to prevent anticipation. When Champ is doing a full power recall consistently, begin adding a front sit here occasionally.

When the full heeling pattern is attentive and accurate, introduce the left about turn. Continue to work on the right about turns, however, to keep Champ smooth and close.

277

Separate the retrieve and teach this exercise by itself until Champ has a functional motivational retrieve. Add it into the routine only when all the other exercises are on their way to being polished.

<u>Training Sessions</u>

Once you are working on all the exercises, practice only some at each session. A typical session might include (in order):

– two heeling patterns, sit in motion, down in motion, front sit from one or two paces, one finish (if front sit is perfect), down in place (without build-up heeling), motivational recall (no front sit) with play after.

– one heeling pattern, moving sit, moving down, three or four front sits, down in place (no build-up heeling), motivational recall, play, voraus with play after.

– one heeling pattern, moving sit, moving down, one front sit, three or four finishes, down in place, recall with front sit (no finish), play after.

– two heeling patterns, moving sit, moving down with motivational recall, play, voraus with play after.

– one heeling pattern, retrieve, jumping practice.

– one heeling pattern, moving sit, moving down, one front, one finish, down in place, motivational recall, play, voraus with play after.

– two heeling patterns, moving sit, moving down with motivational recall, play, retrieve on flat, voraus with play.

– one heeling pattern, moving sit, moving down, recall with front sit, finish (if sit is perfect), play, voraus with play after.

– two heeling patterns, retrieve on flat and over jumps.

Alternate between a recall with front sit and jumping into the hose (motivational recall), depending on what your dog needs most – control or *motivation*. Add the finish occasionally, and **only** when the first front sit is perfect.

When leaving Champ on the down, **always** return and feed him at least once before going the full distance (preferably further) for the recall.

The combination of exercises is flexible, depending on each dog's *drive*, fitness, enthusiasm, training level and individual characteristics (not to mention the trainer's threshold and energy level).

The reason for working on only part of the routine in each training session is that we want Champ to work with full power in every exercise. This way you stop before your dog loses that full power.

It is not possible for any dog always to perform the complete routine with full power. We want training to teach Champ to work in *drive* for each exercise, so we keep sessions very short to insure his enjoyment and enthusiasm.

If any major problem arises with any particular exercise, work on that exercise (or portion of the exercise) by itself (**Foundation**), away from the training field. Add it back into the routine when it is stabilized by itself.

Adding Exercises

When adding the retrieve to the pattern, keep any repetitions of other exercises to a minimum. Include the retrieve only on days when previous exercises are short and successful. Follow the retrieve with fun jumping (no retrieve), or with a motivational voraus (clearly visible target) followed by play.

When adding the stands, **always** practice all four motion exercises together in proper sequence. At this level, decide which **half** of the routine to practice. For SchH. III, a typical session might include:
– one heeling pattern, all four motion exercises (no recall after running stand), motivational voraus with play after.
– heeling, retrieve on flat and over jumps, voraus with play after.

Whenever you prepare for a voraus without a recall, especially on a new field, **show** Champ where you are tossing the hose before sending him. Or use a visible target.

At the end of any recall, turn Champ down the field (in the direction he runs on the voraus), and hold his collar. Toss the hose a few feet away to set him up for the voraus. Occasionally, you can only **pretend** to toss the hose there.

Add a retrieve in between the recall and voraus **only** when Champ is consistently charging out to the recall spot. Or return to using a visible target. Also, be sure to throw the dumbbell in the **opposite** direction from the recall and voraus.

New exercises can be taught separately and individually, on or off the field, or at home. When teaching any new exercise, limit your repetitions to three or four. **Always** end with success, even if you have to back up several steps to do so.

Avoid the "One-More-Time Syndrome." When Champ gets it right, even on the first or second try, quit there. If he makes a mistake on that "one more time," you'll have to try again, or back up a step to end with success.

When adding a new exercise to the pattern, keep the rest of the routine short and simple. Practice finishes **only** on a day when the **first** front sit is perfect.

Two or three repetitions of any exercise is usually enough. If the first one is perfect, move on to the next exercise.

If the second or third repetition does not improve, back up a step and get that sequence right. Prevent your dog from making a mistake twice in a row. Resolve to work more on that exercise separately or in the next session.

If you must work in hot weather, keep everything short and quit **before** your dog gets hot or tired. While tracking might possibly be productive even in the heat, obedience work only teaches your dog that it is not so much fun.

Working in real heat can also be dangerous. Heat stroke can occur if your dog really works in *drive* and expends lots of energy. On a hot day, always allow Champ plenty of time to cool down before putting him away.

If you notice your dog getting tired or stressed during any training session, do something simple and end on success. When doing several exercises, end **every** session with play at the location of the last motivational exercise (recall or voraus).

After training, play only **on** the training field, not off. We want Champ to consider the training field the **most** fun place to be.

Playing on the field at the **end** of each session:
– increases Champ's fitness level each time,
– gives him a positive attitude to the training field and,
– leaves him wanting **more**.

Field Trips

The basic routines are practiced the same way on the same field for some time, until Champ's **Foundation** is fully functional on a familiar field. When taking him to a new place, go back to basics.

Allow him to look around and sniff. **Wait** until he is bored and ready to work. (See Figs. 7 to 10, Page 54.)

Then add **more** *motivation* to make yourself more interesting than the surroundings. Ignore any unwanted behavior, but *reward* **all** desired responses, especially **Attention.**

Abbreviate the routine just to heeling and then play. The next time you go to a new field, add one or two of Champ's favorite exercises (recall and voraus). On any new field, **play** two hoses more than train. Add **more** food to each exercise.

Make yourself exciting to Champ. Teach him that new places mean more fun, not corrections!

Reinforcement Regimen

For **Foundation** work, teach each exercise with **constant** *positive reinforcement*. Progress to constant *reward*. Create the correct habit by making Champ believe he gets what he wants **every** time his behavior is correct.

Introduce the command only **when** Champ is in the proper position. Repeat the command only **while** Champ remains in this position.

During **Foundation** work, avoid using the command when your dog is not in correct position. To your dog, this only connects the command with the **wrong** response.

For example, say Heel only when Champ is in perfect heel position as you feed. Say Sit only when Champ is sitting correctly while you feed him.

Making Champ believe he gets what he wants **every** time he is correct is the key to motivational training. This is what makes the *imprint* for intense **Attention**, perfect **Accuracy** and an enthusiastic **Attitude**.

Building such a **Foundation** takes time because you allow Champ to think for himself and figure out what is right. This time is certainly well spent, however, when Champ bounces back from a rare correction with his great **Attitude** still intact.

<u>Trial Preparation</u>

Once Champ has a truly functional **Foundation**, and **Polishing** and proofing are nearly complete, you are ready to prepare for trial. Return to your familiar field.

Practice the same preparation you plan to use for the trial. Now psyche Champ up and get him excited **off** the field.

Practice reporting in, first without another dog-handler team next to you. Reinforce his **Attention** with food.

Also keep Champ's **Attention** by stroking his chin to avoid him sniffing or looking around. You have already let him look around **before** he came on the field.

Practice the Attention Sit with Champ for longer periods of time before exercises. *Reward* with food or release. This prepares him for waiting for the judge between exercises.

On days when Champ is especially excited and enthusiastic, begin **random** *positive reinforcement* and *reward*. Now you wean Champ from constant food and practice **some** parts of the exercises without it.

Return to **constant** feeding the next session. Begin to vary when Champ gets continual feeding, and where he must work a little longer for it.

The week of the trial, however, end with one or two sessions full of constant *positive reinforcement* and *reward*, just as you did in **Foundation** training for each exercise. This restores Champ's belief that he **always** gets what he wants when he is correct, and that he can drive you for it.

Trial preparation is distinctly different from training. It is a book in itself. So is correct, productive handling. But there are some basics.

A good general rule is no obedience training for two days before a trial. This usually helps Champ arrive at the field **wanting** to work. (It also eliminates the possibility of creating a problem you can't fix in one day!)

This does depend on your dog's individual temperament, however. If he's crazy rather than lazy, you may want to continue training if that works better.

On the actual trial field, by now you probably only need to play hoses with Champ down the center line and at the end of the field where he will do his recall and voraus (positive *place association*), and let him go over the jump once or twice. If **you** need to do more, practice one recall and one voraus in the direction they will be performed in the trial.

Then put Champ away, or on a long down if you have someone to watch him and the field is not too busy with other dogs and handlers. You now walk the pattern by yourself to be sure **you** know what to do, when and where. If you do your part, Champ usually does his.

Trial Tips

In the trial, assume your basic position before each exercise by walking **straight** down the center line to your designated starting place. Several steps before, have Champ heeling correctly. Then halt at your starting place.

From correct heeling, Champ's sit is correct the **first** time. This avoids the pivoting and repositioning which breaks Champ's (and your) concentration.

Once in basic position, take a deep breath and smile! This calms you and reduces stress. Take this moment to think and plan this next exercise. Avoid being in a hurry.

If at any point you seem to be losing your dog's attention, simply speed up and walk **faster.** Turning to look at him only encourages lagging, especially in the group.

Use the release after each exercise to **energize** Champ. Act confident and positive so he knows you have everything under control.

At the jump, position yourself so that Champ can take **two** comfortable strides before jumping. Aim to throw the dumbbell approximately the same distance on the other side.

Realize that you cannot keep your dog at peak trial performance all the time. When you set a date to trial, arrange your training schedule to allow time to prepare Champ's performance properly.

After a trial, return immediately to higher *motivation* and more play in your next few training sessions. If you can play hoses on that same field after the trial, even better. Convince Champ that those odd times he doesn't get what he wants are just a fluke.

Traveling is stressful for most of us, dogs and people alike. Allow Champ plenty of "doggie down time" before the trial.

Stop physical conditioning four to six days prior to the trial. Save his energy for his performance. Substitute long walks in the fields or woods where you can let your dog be a dog, without any nagging or pressure. Throw the hoses only a few times, leaving him **really** wanting more.

Keep his schedule and environment as close to home as possible. If he's a house dog, allow him free time rather than keeping him in a crate constantly. And be careful not to spoil a kennel dog by allowing him too much freedom on the road or in the motel.

Take your regular food and water with you. On the road, feed slightly less than normal rations. Cut his ration by one-half the meal prior to the trial, whether morning or evening.

Pleasant Surprise

Your dog is sure to surprise you on trial day. Watch for signs of him thinking, figuring it all out.

All us skeptics have been converted by watching one of our motivationally trained dogs put together amazing thought sequences in a trial. They show not only that they understand, but they **want** to do what they have been taught! Watch for these moments – they are so rewarding.

To truly understand your relationship with your dog, evaluate it honestly and decide what you give to each other. Our dogs are sensitive partners who show us concern, cooperation, commitment, courage and compassion.

Share what you have with your dog. Respect him for all that he is and all that he gives.

What we have provided here is only a guideline. Be creative within this framework. Stay flexible, but adhere to the principles. Take into account your dog's individual character.

Be innovative. Discover **what works** with your dog. Find out what stimulates his drives to create **Attention, Accuracy** and **Attitude**.

Each dog teaches us something new. We are striving to be graduates of the Whatever Works (Best) School of Dog Training. Should you discover or expand a technique that works consistently, we hope you'll share it with us.

Let's help each other toward the day when we can all say we are "**Having fun now!**" training our wonderful dogs.

GLOSSARY

anthropomorphism - the attribution of human motives, characteristics or emotions to animals.

behavior – the manifestation of a dog's temperament.

condition - a dog's overall well-being and state of health, primarily physical, but affects and includes mental health.

drive - an exaggerated instinctual response to certain stimuli and situations, often breed specific. (an enhanced instinct.)

Drives vs. Instincts:

Certain instincts are common to all canines (wolf and dog specifically). These include a wide range of response behaviors such as licking, chewing, vocalizing, digging, mounting, leg-lifting and scratching. Instincts most often have their roots in survival or reproduction.

Drives have their beginnings as instincts, but are more developed and usually more breed specific (ie: retrieving drive in hunters, herding drive in sheepdogs, fight drive in guarding breeds). Most drives, unlike instincts, can be built or heightened if they are present. Conversely, they can also be suppressed and often even extinguished, unlike instincts. Thus is it usually easier to get a dog to stop retrieving or herding than it is to stop him licking, scratching or digging.

A simple way of understanding the difference between the two is that the dog's drive determines the degree to which he exhibits instinctive behavior. So while it is instinctive for a dog to salivate and eat, food drive determines how often, how eagerly and how intensely he pursues food.

To chase a running cat is instinctive, but how persistently depends on prey drive. To chase a ball relies on certain hunting instincts, but to pick the ball up and continually return to you with it shows developed retrieving drive. For a dog to amuse himself with the ball demands play drive.

Thus it may be instinctive for a dog to startle or bark at a stranger in its territory, but the dog's fight drive controls his behavior and his persistence in any conflict. The degree to which any dog exhibits his drives depends on other factors in his temperament.

emotional sensitivity - a dog's reaction (temperament) and response (behavior) to the mood, feelings and demeanor of his handler.

energy level - a dog's desire to be active. Activity can be prompted by both drive (positive) or nervousness (negative).

food drive - a dog's desire to persist in getting food, not always related to hunger or the biological need for food.

fight drive - a dog's desire to initiate and persist in confrontation, both physical and mental.

hardness - a dog's ability to withstand negative stimulation and remain unaffected. the ability to bounce back in drive. (A correction in obedience requires resiliency in pack drive, as well as in whichever drive is being used. A helper's threat requires resiliency in fight drive. Each drive has its own hardness factor for each dog. Thus the same dog may be able to withstand a certain degree of negative stimulation in prey drive, but not in fight drive.)

imprint - a dog's first, lasting impression of a situation or stimulus.

instinct - a dog's innate response to certain stimuli, independent of any thought process and common to all canine species.

motivation - attracting a dog by providing something he wants which stimulates him into the desired response.

nerve strength - a dog's inner core of confidence (temperament) which creates his ability to react (behavior) calmly and clearly to external stimuli.

nervousness - a dog's tendency to worry (temperament) and thereby overreact (behavior) to external stimuli.

opposition reflex - a dog's tendency to resist and move against physical pressure, rather than succumb.

pack drive - a dog's desire to work with the handler and be a member of a team.

place association - a dog's tendency to first connect a stimulus or experience with the location where it happens, and continues to happen.

play drive - a dog's obsession with objects and his desire to entertain himself actively.

positive reinforcement - adding something to training (preferably **during** or immediately after a behavior), which increases the frequency, intensity or duration of that behavior in response to a certain stimulus.

prey drive - a dog's intensity in chasing anything moving (primarily away), including catching, biting and carrying it.

punishment - adding something to training which diminshes the frequency, intensity or duration of a specific behavior.

reward - providing something the dog likes, or causes pleasure, **after** he has completed a specific action.

shaping - offering positive reinforcement for each small movement toward desired behavior.

stamina - a dog's ability to continue activity and resist fatigue when motivated or stimulated physically or mentally.

temperament - the combination of all a dog's mental and emotional attributes, which dictates how he perceives his environment and causes his actions and reactions (behavior).

PHOTO IDENTIFICATION

(All photos by Sheila Booth unless otherwise noted.)

FIG.	PAGE	IDENTIFICATION
1	xvi	Espe von der Kolonie SchH. III, FH, IPO III, CD, KKlsse. Ia and Countryhaus Charra SchH. III, KKlsse. II, AD (USDAA Agility Dog), EAC (NADAC Elite Agility Certificate).
2	6	Bridget vom Stolzenfels SchH. I and Mark Tyler of Bloomfield, CT.
3	24	Quindy von der Eisenkaute SchH. I and Debbie Zappia of Macedon, NY.
4, 5	32	Quindy and Debbie Zappia.
6	42	Hannah Bell Am./Can. CDX owned by Loel Turpin of Geneseo, NY.
7-10	54	Countryhaus Orio ("Rio") Police K-9 N.Y. State Certified for Patrol, Tracking and Drug Detection, U.S.P.C.A. Certified for Drug Detection and Sgt. Rick Kemner of East Greenbush, NY.
11, 12	71	V Natan vom Schontratal SchH. III, Kklsse. Ia and Debbie Zappia.
13, 14	74	Rio and Rick Kemner.
15	76	Rio and Rick Kemner.

FIG.	PAGE	IDENTIFICATION
16, 17	77	Cliff von Geiersnest SchH. III, IPO III and Joanne Plumb of Loretta, Ontario, Canada
18, 19	108	Natan and Debbie Zappia.
20	112	Bridget and Mark Tyler.
21	116	Belinda vom Jordheim SchH. I and Rick Kemner. *(Photo by Cheryl Heath.)*
22	117	Igor vom Lowenfels SchH. III and Mary Lou Hall of Lady Lake, FL.
23	118	Igor and Mary Lou Hall. *(Photo by George Ardner.)*
24	122	Tucker vom Stolzenfels SchH. I, CD and Jody Potter of Windsor, CT.
25	122	Natan and Debbie Zappia.
26	127	Minx vom Leerburg and Jody Potter.
27	127	Natan and Debbie Zappia.
28	130	Quindy and Debbie Zappia.
29	134	Uran vom Rolandsbogen SchH. III, KKlsse. Ia and Dennis Smar of Tylersport, PA.
30-33	137	Bridget and Mark Tyler.
34	148	Espe.

FIG.	PAGE	IDENTIFICATION
35, 36	151	Minx.
37	153	Bridget and Mark Tyler.
38	166	Igor and Mary Lou Hall.
39, 40	169	Tucker and Jody Potter.
41, 42	169	Natan and Debbie Zappia.
43-45	171	Rio and Rick Kemner.
46-48	176	Natan and Debbie Zappia.
49	188	Natan and Debbie Zappia.
50-53	190	Natan and Debbie Zappia.
54, 55	191	Natan and Debbie Zappia.
56	198	Countryhaus Carma.
57, 58	210	Uran and Dennis Smar.
59	213	Hiasl vom Wildsteiger Land SchH. III and Jackie Reinhart of Fort McCoy, FL.
60	214	Igor and Mary Lou Hall. (*Photo by George Ardner.*)
61	217	Briarwood's K-Arri SchH. I and Lavonda Herring of Lagrangeville, NY.
62	222	Igor. (*Photo by John Thompson.*)

FIG.	PAGE	IDENTIFICATION
63	224	Banner von der König SchH.III, FH, WH, CDX, TD and Sue King of Ocala, FL.
64	224	Igor. (*Photo by John Thompson.*)
65	227	Espe.
66	229	Olgameister's Nadia.
67	230	Uran vom Haus Sahrig and Dil Luther of Deltona, FL.
68-70	234	Tucker and Jody Potter.
71-73	235	Tucker and Jody Potter.
74	256	Uran and Dennis Smar.
75	274	From Left: 3rd Place –Banjo vom Schwarzen Baeran SchH. III (Bouvier) and Joanne Plumb; 1st Place – Igor (Malinois) and Mary Lou Hall; 2nd Place – V Niko von der Hochantenne SchH. III, KKlsse. Ia (GSD) and Jackie Reinhart on the podium at the 1990 DVG National Championship in Miami. (All three winners coached by Gottfried Dildei.)

COACH GOTTFRIED DILDEI CONGRATULATES
JACKIE REINHART, FIRST AMERICAN TO WIN
THE DEUTSCHE MEISTERSCHAFT (1988 & 1989).

ABOUT GOTTFRIED DILDEI

Purchasing his first dog at the age of 12, Gottfried began a 30-year involvement in the dog sport. His dedication would lead him, four years later, to receive his DVG Helper Certification and, by the following year, to have trained two dogs to SchH. III. But that was just the beginning.

The years 1974 through 1978 saw him win the DVG LV Championship four consecutive times, place second once, be SV, LV, FH Sieger, and SchH. III Sieger, be responsible for second place once in the ADRK Deutsche Meister and become the youngest ever DVG Judge at that time. He competed in the Bundessieger and Deutsche Meisterschaft a total of seven times, and in 1983 he placed fourth in the latter.

As an executive member of the Landesgruppe, he held the positions of Counsellor and Trainer for the LG Youth Organization and LG Trainer. Gottfried has been Training Director for four clubs and was directly responsible for training two helpers and five dog-handler teams who have all participated in the Deutsche Meisterschaft.

For 11 years, he worked for a large security company, where his duties included training dog-handler teams, testing and purchasing dogs, and placing dogs for the German Army.

Gottfried immigrated to Canada in 1984, where he was responsible for several dog-handler teams who participated in the DVG Nationals in Florida (1987) and St. Louis (1988), with one of those teams winning the SchH. I Championship and another placing fourth in the SchH. III Qualification. He was instrumental in the formation of the KG North, where he held the position of President until his move to Florida in the fall of 1989.

Gottfried also contributed greatly to the success of Niko v.d. Hochantenne SchH. III (GSD), owned and handled by Jackie Reinhart, and Igor vom Lowenfels SchH. III (Malinois), owned and handled by Mary Lou Brayman. Both dog-handler teams were polished and made trial ready by Gottfried.

As a result, Jackie and Niko won the DVG Nationals in 1988, and the Deutsche Meisterschaft in both 1988 and 1989. This was the first American team to win this event. Jackie was also the first woman to win this, and the first time ever that someone won it two consecutive years!

Mary Lou and Igor have enjoyed equal success under Gottfried's guidance. In 1990, this team won their KG Championship, the DVG Nationals in Florida, and then went on to win the Deutsche Meisterschaft in Germany. In 1991, Mary Lou and Igor again won the DVG Nationals. The team that stood in second place that same year was another team that Gottfried had coached: Joanne Plumb and Cliff vom Geiersnest SchH. III, IPO III.

Gottfried now lives in Central Florida where he imports and breeds dogs at his Grauen Wolf Kennels, sells equipment, and runs GDIT (Gottfried Dildei Innovative Training) Training Centre – (352) 330-0055. www.GDIT.com. There he is involved with all aspects of the dog sport, always striving for the betterment of the training and the dog.

OWNER-HANDLER SHEILA BOOTH WITH ESPE AFTER
WINNING THE 1987 DVG SE REGIONAL CHAMPIONSHIP
WITH 298 (100-98-100) IN FT. LAUDERDALE, FLORIDA.

ABOUT SHEILA BOOTH

A hard-headed yellow Lab launched Sheila into dog training while still a college student in California. Aptly named, Gypsy was so independent that she jumped through picture windows and killed chickens right in front of her distressed owner. Dog training became a necessity!

Born in England and raised in Canada and Connecticut, Sheila had already acquired a great love and respect for all animals from her European parents. Early in her career as a trainer, she chose to ask "Why?" and began studying animal behavior and wolf ethology for greater understanding and insight.

After college, Sheila discovered AKC obedience competition and Gypsy eventually became a High In Trial contender. Her next dog was a marvelously sensitive Standard Poodle, Ebony, whom she trained through Utility. He also won High In Trial honors, while providing a breath of fresh air after the challenge of training Gypsy.

In 1975, Sheila discovered Schutzhund. Yes, she began training in the sport with that Standard Poodle. Her first real success came with a Belgian Tervuren – Am./Can. Champion Quintessence de Chateau Blanc SchH. III, CD. Tessa earned her SchH. III with High In Trial honors, competed in two DVG National Championships and also earned V-ratings more than once in every phase of the sport, including multiple 100 points in tracking.

Espe von der Kolonie, a female German Shepherd, came to Sheila in 1985. She was already titled to SchH. II, but a clear training victim, suffering from the use of far too much compulsion.

After two years of purely motivational training, Espe became the top ranked Schutzhund dog in America that year. Also in 1987, at the DVG Southeast Regional Championship in Florida, this team earned one of the highest scores ever posted in this country: 298 (100-98-100).

Espe also placed second at the USA National Championship in St. Louis that same year and was reserve member of the USA team for the WUSV Championship in Switzerland. Espe also V-rated more than once in every category, including 100 points in both tracking and protection and earned 95 points in FH.

Sheila then titled an Espe daughter, Countryhaus Charra, to SchH. III, also with V-ratings in every category and 100 points in tracking. Charra retired from Schutzhund competition at 8 years old and went on to a career in agility. She won numerous blue ribbons there and finished her Elite Agility title (the top level) at 12 years young.

Agility is Sheila's new passion and her Belgian Malinois, Vino, has earned the prestigious Agility Dog Championship title and competed at two National Championships.

Sheila served as New England Regional Director for the defunct North American Working Dog Association (NASA) and for the USA organization. For many years, she was Training Director of the very successful Upstate Schutzhund Club, just outside Albany, NY. Sheila also ran a full-service kennel in New York state, where she specialized in obedience training and behavior consultations, especially for aggression management. She taught obedience classes and private lessons for more than 10 years.

With a background as a professional horse trainer and riding instructor (hunters, dressage and eventing), Sheila now prefers to ride for pleasure and to condition her dogs (much to their delight). She has been invited to give seminars in Australia, South America, Europe and South Africa, but prefers to spend her time at home in Connecticut with her beloved dogs. She gives one public seminar each year in the U.S., coaches a few teams in Schutzhund, and perfects her dogs' talents in the sport of agility.

Sheila earned her journalism degree in California, after attending Emerson College in Boston. She wrote a weekly dog column for a chain of newspapers in Connecticut for several years, and is a popular speaker on dog behavior at a variety of conferences. She has been editor of newspapers in both Connecticut and New York, as well as a contributor to Dog Sports Magazine, DVG America, Schutzhund USA and Clean Run, the national agility magazine.

ACKNOWLEDGEMENTS

"Thank You" to:

My family, *without whose financial and personal support this book would not be possible.* Specifically,

My parents, Frank and Edna, *for endowing me with their great love and respect for all animals and for understanding the slightly off-center lifestyle of a dog trainer and writer.*

My brother David and his wife Marilyn, *for believing in me enough to stake their hard-earned money on me.*

My friend Mary Lou Brayman, *for sharing Schutzhund and making it more fun!*

Rick Kemner, *whose support made this book possible.*

All those who helped me grow as a trainer – especially Margo Craig, Kae Reilley, Wendy and Jack Volhard, and Edgar Kaltenbach.

Carlene Jarvis, *for introducing me to Schutzhund and the qualities of the German Shepherd Dog.*

And special *"Thanks"* to:

Gottfried Dildei, *for opening my eyes, testing my mettle, inspiring my creative productivity, and helping me bring two worlds together.*

All my students, *who surely taught me much more than I ever did them,* and

Gypsy, *for making me a dog trainer so many years ago, and all my subsequent dogs – my very best friends.*

— Sheila Booth

ACKNOWLEDGEMENTS

"Thank You" to:

My family, *for all their support.* Specifically,
My wife, Ingrid, *for all that she did to allow me
to pursue this training.*
Robyn and David, *for all their hard work.*
My daughter, Kirstin, *for her understanding.*

My friend, Klaus Huber, *for first introducing me to
motivational training and inspiring me to develop
these techniques.*

And special *"Thanks"* to:
Sheila Booth, *whose excellent organization and writing skills
finally allowed me to put into words what I want to be
available to everyone to read and understand, not only
for Schutzhund, but for our dogs and training in
general.*

All those who worked with me, believed in these training
methods and trusted my guidance, especially Jackie
Reinhart, Mary Lou Brayman and Joanne Plumb *for
their dedication to using my techniques so we could
reach the top together.*

— Gottfried Dildei

xxxii